CW00970963

Their Morals and Ours

Their Morals and Ours

The class foundations of moral practice

Leon Trotsky

PATHFINDER

NEW YORK LONDON MONTREAL SYDNEY

IN MEMORY OF LEON SEDOV
1906-1938

ISBN 0-87348-319-7 (paper); 0-87348-318-9 (cloth)
Library of Congress Catalog Card Number 73-82168
Manufactured in the United States of America

Fifth edition, 1973
Fifth printing, 1992

Pathfinder

410 West Street, New York, NY 10014, U.S.A.

Pathfinder distributors around the world:
Australia (and Asia and the Pacific):
  Pathfinder, 19 Terry St., Surry Hills, Sydney, N.S.W. 2010
Britain (and Europe, Africa except South Africa, and Middle East):
  Pathfinder, 47 The Cut, London, SE1 8LL
Canada:
  Pathfinder, 6566, boul. St-Laurent, Montreal, Quebec, H2S 3C6
Iceland:
  Pathfinder, Klapparstíg 26, 2d floor, 121 Reykjavík
New Zealand:
  Pathfinder, La Gonda Arcade, 203 Karangahape Road, Auckland
  Postal address: P.O. Box 8730, Auckland
Sweden:
  Pathfinder, Vikingagatan 10, S-113 42, Stockholm
United States (and Caribbean, Latin America, and South Africa):
  Pathfinder, 410 West Street, New York, NY 10014

Contents

About the Authors

Leon Trotsky (1879-1940) was a leader of the Bolshevik Party, which led the Russian toilers to victory in the October 1917 revolution that brought landlord and capitalist rule to an end. He was a central leader of the new workers' and peasants' republic, the Russian Communist Party, and the Communist International (Comintern) during its first five  years. As commissar of war, he helped guide the Red Army to victory during three years of civil war and imperialist intervention.

From Lenin's final illness in mid-1923, Trotsky was the principal leader of the communist forces in the leadership of the party who fought to continue Lenin's course in the face of the rising privileged petty-bourgeois social layer whose spokesman came to be Joseph Stalin. Trotsky was expelled from the party and, in 1929, driven into exile. In 1933, after Hitler took power with no resistance organized by the Communist Party in Germany, Trotsky concluded that the Comintern had been irrevocably transformed into a counterrevolutionary instrument within the working-class movement, and called for building a new revolutionary international.

Trotsky was the main defendant, in absentia, at the 1936-38 frame-up trials in Moscow. He was assassinated at his home in Mexico in 1940 by an agent of Stalin's secret police.

John Dewey (1859-1952) was the most influential proponent in the United States of the philosophical school of pragmatism, which he developed into his own outlook of "instrumentalism." Dewey was a prominent political commentator, education

4

theorist, and standard-bearer of liberalism in the first half of the twentieth century.

Widely respected for his personal integrity, Dewey served as chairman of the 1937 Commission of Inquiry into the Charges Made against Leon Trotsky in the Moscow Trials. In a major blow to Stalin's frame-up, the Dewey Commission investigated and rejected the frame-up charges.

George Novack (1905-) joined the communist movement in the United States in 1933 and for six decades has been a member and leader of the Socialist Workers Party.

As national secretary of the American Committee for the Defense of Leon Trotsky, Novack helped organize the 1937 International Commission of Inquiry that investigated the charges fabricated by Stalin's Moscow trials. In the 1940s Novack was national secretary of the Civil Rights Defense Committee, which gathered support for leaders of the SWP and General Drivers Local 544 in Minnesota framed up as the first victims of the witch-hunting anticommunist Smith Act. He played a prominent role in numerous other civil liberties battles over subsequent decades.

Novack is the author of a number of books on political theory and history, including *Understanding History, Democracy and Revolution*, and *Pragmatism versus Marxism*, a critical appraisal of John Dewey's views.

Introduction

Leon Trotsky was the central organizer of the Red Army during the Russian civil war, which raged from 1918 to 1921, when the first socialist revolution was threatened by the intervention of imperialist armies as well as by counterrevolution. During this period, Trotsky became known as the foremost defender, in the military arena, of socialist revolution.

In *Their Morals and Ours* we see Trotsky as an equally effective combatant in the arena of moral ideas. This classic defense of revolutionary morality is directed at those disillusioned intellectuals of the thirties who attempted to rationalize their departure from revolutionary Marxism with the argument that some abstract notion of morality, and not the necessities of the class struggle, should be the guiding principle for those who attempt to create more rational and humane circumstances of life.

This argument was not new when it was advanced in the thirties, and it has been repeated since that time in many different forms. But subsequent events have stressed the importance of Trotsky's analysis of these critics of socialist revolution, emphasizing the validity of his revolutionary conclusions: "Only that which prepares the complete and final overthrow of imperialist bestiality is moral, and nothing else. The welfare of the revolution — that is the supreme law!"

Trotsky begins *Their Morals and Ours* by pointing to the effects of "an epoch of triumphant reaction" on

7

backsliding intellectuals and representatives of radical political currents. The rise of fascism in Germany had been the opening round in this triumph of reaction. In 1933 Hitler gained control of the state apparatus and proceeded to crush the last remaining organs of working class power — all without any serious opposition from the powerful Communist and Socialist parties.

Hitler's victory made the threat of fascism an immediate reality to people around the world. The Communist and Socialist parties advocated building coalitions with liberal bourgeois parties as a defense against this threat. In practice this policy led to subordinating the workers' organizations to those of the bourgeoisie. The Popular Front dissipated the revolutionary aspirations of the French workers in the mid-thirties. But it was in Spain that the tragic effects of Popular Frontism were most crushingly realized. The revolutionary Spanish workers and peasants were prevented by their own leadership from taking power and decisively eliminating the fascist threat. By 1938, when *Their Morals and Ours* was written, Franco was in the process of cutting Republican Spain in half; total fascist victory was only a short time away.

Millions who looked to the Communist International and the Soviet Union for leadership were disoriented by evidence of the repressive measures Stalin employed against his working class opponents. By the mid-thirties, nearly all of the prominent oppositionists had been exiled, imprisoned, or murdered by Stalin's secret police. Following 1935, Stalin swept the country with periodic purges. This campaign of terror was elevated to the level of official policy in August 1936 when Stalin staged the first Moscow trial. Among the accused were such leading Bolsheviks as Zinoviev, Kamenev, and Smirnov. This trial was followed in January 1937 by a second one involving Pyatakov, Radek, and Muralov. In March 1938, Bukharin, Rykov, and other prominent Bolsheviks were put on trial, as well as secret-police chief Yagoda, chief organizer of the first trial.

"Stalin renders a commendable service to fascism," Mussolini declared concerning this last spectacle (*Popolo d'Italia*). For Stalin had wiped out the entire leadership of the Russian Revolution. In 1937 Stalin topped off these services to reaction by shooting the leadership of the Red Army, including Marshal Tukhachevsky, without even a pretense of an open trial. This act militarily weakened the first workers' state at a time when all the other European powers were rapidly rearming.

The most important targets of the Moscow show trials were Trotsky and his son Leon Sedov. In order to give Trotsky the opportunity to answer Stalin's charges before world opinion, a Commission of Inquiry chaired by the eminent American philosopher John Dewey was formed, held hearings in Mexico, and examined all the evidence in the case. Although the frame-up charges were easily disproved before the Dewey Commission, they were supported by the resources of the Soviet state and slavishly affirmed by powerful political forces in every major country.

Meanwhile, World War II was on the horizon, providing an increasingly threatening backdrop to these events. Hitler's rapid rearmament of Germany produced a reflex strengthening of patriotic sentiments in Europe and America. Trotsky and the movement he led continued to call for the mobilization of the working class against both fascism and the impending world war. But they were virtually alone. The radical intellectuals — who had previously defended Trotsky and the Russian Revolution — were thrown into a state of confusion.

Figures like Sidney Hook, Max Eastman, Victor Serge, and Boris Souvarine had already begun to disavow Leninism. Although not identical, their case histories had certain points in common. During an upswing in the radicalization, they supported and popularized the ideas of Marxism; but during a period of "triumphant reaction," they became the leading conveyors of demoralization into the revolutionary movement. By 1938 it was obvious that the negative side of their dual role was predominant. Rather than make concessions to these "carriers of infection," Trotsky called for "a completely thought-out inflexible rupture from the philosophy not only of the big but of the petty bourgeoisie."

All but a few of the disillusioned intellectuals of the thirties supported the imperialist governments in their countries during World War II. Some, like Hook and Eastman, drifted from liberalism to conservatism — a striking verification of Trotsky's estimate that their moralism was "a bridge from revolution to reaction."

In the process of their break with revolutionary Marxism, they raised the claim that Stalinism was simply an outgrowth of Bolshevism. Whether or not they had defended Trotsky against Stalin's crude frame-up charges, the ex-Trotskyists and ex-Stalinists alike, along with the Social Democrats and liberals, used the Moscow trials as an opportunity to equate the "police morality of Stalinism with the revolutionary morality of the Bolsheviks," of which Trotsky was the only prominent survivor.

Written in Mexico, his last place of exile, *Their Morals and Ours* is Trotsky's response to these charges. Shortly after completing it he learned of the death of Leon Sedov, to whom he dedicated this essay. It appeared first in the Russian language *Bulletin of the Opposition* and then in the June 1938 *New International. The Moralists and Sycophants Against Marxism,* written sixteen months later, takes up criticisms of *Their Morals and Ours,* including those contained in a prospectus to Victor Serge's French translation (the appendix to this volume contains that prospectus as well as Serge's denial and Trotsky's reply). Minor corrections in the translation of the two Trotsky essays have been made for this edition.

Pressing political obligations prevented Trotsky from responding to the essay included here by John Dewey, entitled *Means and Ends,* which appeared in the August 1938 *New International.* The Marxist scholar George Novack, who had been the national secretary of the American Committee for the Defense of Leon Trotsky, reviews the debated issues and brings them up to date in his essay *Liberal Morality,* first published in the Fall 1965 *International Socialist Review.*

July 1973   DAVID SALNER

Their Morals and Ours
by Leon Trotsky

Moral effluvia

During an epoch of triumphant reaction, Messrs. Democrats, Social Democrats, Anarchists, and other representatives of the "left" camp begin to exude double their usual amount of moral effluvia, similar to persons who perspire doubly in fear. Paraphrasing the Ten Commandments or the Sermon on the Mount, these moralists address themselves not so much to triumphant reaction as to those revolutionists suffering under its persecution, who with their "excesses" and "amoral" principles "provoke" reaction and give it moral justification. Moreover they prescribe a simple but certain means of avoiding reaction: It is necessary only to strive and morally to regenerate oneself. Free samples of moral perfection for those desirous are furnished by all the interested editorial offices.

The class basis of this false and pompous sermon is the intellectual petty bourgeoisie. The political basis — their impotence and confusion in the face of approaching reaction. Psychological basis — their effort at overcoming the feeling of their own inferiority through masquerading in the beard of a prophet.

A moralizing philistine's favorite method is the lumping of reaction's conduct with that of revolution. He achieves success in this device through recourse to formal analogies. To him czarism and Bolshevism* are twins. Twins are likewise discovered in fascism and communism. An inventory is compiled of the common features in Catholicism — or more specifically, Jesuitism — and Bolshevism. Hitler and Mussolini, utilizing from their side exactly

---

*See Glossary for names and terms such as Bolshevism.

13

the same method, disclose that liberalism, democracy, and Bolshevism represent merely different manifestations of one and the same evil. The conception that Stalinism and Trotskyism are "essentially" one and the same now enjoys the joint approval of liberals, democrats, devout Catholics, idealists, pragmatists, anarchists and fascists. If the Stalinists are unable to adhere to this "People's Front," then it is only because they are accidentally occupied with the extermination of Trotskyists.

The fundamental feature of these approximations and similitudes lies in their completely ignoring the material foundation of the various currents, that is, their class nature and by that token their objective historical role. Instead they evaluate and classify different currents according to some external and secondary manifestation, most often according to their relation to one or another abstract principle which for the given classifier has a special professional value. Thus to the Roman pope, Freemasons and Darwinists, Marxists and anarchists are twins because all of them sacrilegiously deny the immaculate conception. To Hitler, liberalism and Marxism are twins because they ignore "blood and honor." To a democrat, fascism and Bolshevism are twins because they do not bow before universal suffrage, etc., etc.

Undoubtedly the currents grouped above have certain common features. But the gist of the matter lies in the fact that the evolution of humanity exhausts itself neither by universal suffrage, nor by "blood and honor," nor by the dogma of the immaculate conception. The historical process signifies primarily the class struggle; moreover, different classes in the name of different aims may in certain instances utilize similar means. Essentially it cannot be otherwise. Armies in combat are always more or less symmetrical; were there nothing in common in their methods of struggle they could not inflict blows upon each other.

If an ignorant peasant or shopkeeper, understanding neither the origin nor the sense of the struggle between the proletariat and the bourgeoisie, discovers himself between the two fires, he will consider both belligerent camps with equal hatred. And who are all these democratic moralists? Ideologists of intermediary layers who have fallen, or are in fear of falling between the two fires. The chief traits of the prophets of this type are alienation from great historical movements, a hardened conservative mentality, smug narrowness, and a most primitive political cowardice. More than anything, moralists wish that history should leave them in peace with their little books, little magazines, subscribers, common sense, and moral copybooks. But history does not leave them in peace. It cuffs them now from the left, now from the right. Clearly — revolution and reaction, czarism and Bolshevism, communism and fascism, Stalinism and Trotskyism — are all twins. Whoever doubts this may feel the symmetrical skull bumps upon both the right and left sides of these very moralists.

Marxist amoralism and eternal truths

The most popular and most imposing accusation directed against Bolshevik "amoralism" bases itself on the so-called Jesuitical maxim of Bolshevism: "The end justifies the means." From this it is not difficult to reach the further conclusion: Since the Trotskyists, like all Bolsheviks (or Marxists), do not recognize the principles of morality, there is, consequently, no "principled" difference between Trotskyism and Stalinism. Q. E. D.

One completely vulgar and cynical American monthly conducted a questionnaire on the moral philosophy of Bolshevism. The questionnaire, as is customary, was to have simultaneously served the ends of ethics and advertisement. The inimitable H. G. Wells, whose high fancy is surpassed only by his Homeric self-satisfaction, was not slow in solidarizing himself with the reactionary snobs of *Common Sense*. Here everything fell into order. But even those participants who considered it necessary to defend Bolshevism did so, in the majority of cases, not without timid evasions (Eastman): The principles of Marxism are, of course, bad, but among the Bolsheviks there are, nevertheless, worthy people. Truly, such "friends" are more dangerous than enemies.

Should we care to take Messrs. Accusers seriously, then first of all we would ask them: What are your own moral principles? Here is a question that will scarcely receive an answer. Let us admit for the moment that neither personal nor social ends can justify the means. Then it is obviously necessary to seek criteria outside of historical society and those ends which arise in its development. But where? If not on earth, then in the heavens. In divine revelation the priests long ago discovered infallible moral criteria. Petty secular priests speak about eternal moral truths without naming their original source. However, we are justified in concluding: Since these truths are eternal, they should have existed not only before the appearance of half-monkey-half-man upon the earth but before the evolution of the solar system. Whence then did they arise? The theory of eternal morals can in no way survive without God.

Moralists of the Anglo-Saxon type, in so far as they do not confine themselves to rationalist utilitarianism, the ethics of bourgeois bookkeeping, appear conscious or unconscious students of Viscount Shaftesbury, who — at the beginning of the eighteenth century! — deduced moral judgments from a special "moral sense" supposedly once and for all given to humanity. Supraclass morality inevitably leads to the acknowledgment of a special substance, of a "moral sense," "conscience," some kind of absolute, which is nothing more than the cowardly philosophical pseudonym for God. Independent of "ends" — that is, of society — morality, whether we deduce it from eternal truths or from the "nature of man," proves in the end to be a form of "natural theology." Heaven remains the only fortified position for military operations against dialectical materialism.

At the end of the last century in Russia there arose a whole school of "Marxists" (Struve, Berdyaev, Bulgakov, and others) who wished to supplement the teachings of

Marx with a self-sufficient, that is, supraclass moral principle. These people began, of course, with Kant and the categorical imperative. But how did they end? Struve is now a retired minister of the Crimean Baron Wrangel, and a faithful son of the church; Bulgakov is an orthodox priest; Berdyaev expounds the Apocalypse in sundry languages. This metamorphosis, which seems so unexpected at first glance, is not at all explained by the "Slavic soul" — Struve has a German soul — but by the sweep of the social struggle in Russia. The fundamental trend of this metamorphosis is essentially international.

Classical philosophical idealism in so far as it aimed in its time to secularize morality, that is, to free it from religious sanction, represented a tremendous step forward (Hegel). But having torn itself from heaven, moral philosophy had to find earthly roots. To discover these roots was one of the tasks of materialism. After Shaftesbury came Darwin, after Hegel — Marx. To appeal now to "eternal moral truths" signifies attempting to turn the wheels backward. Philosophical idealism is only a stage: from religion to materialism, or, contrariwise, from materialism to religion.

"The end justifies the means"

The Jesuit order, organized in the first half of the sixteenth century for combatting Protestantism, never taught, let it be said, that *any* means, even though it be criminal from the point of view of the Catholic morals, was permissible if only it led to the "end," that is, to the triumph of Catholicism. Such an internally contradictory and psychologically absurd doctrine was maliciously attributed to the Jesuits by their Protestant and partly Catholic opponents, who were not shy in choosing the means for achieving *their own* ends. Jesuit theologians who, like the theologians of other schools, were occupied with the question of personal responsibility, actually taught that the means in itself can be a matter of indifference but that the moral justification or condemnation of the given means flows from the end. Thus shooting in itself is a matter of indifference; shooting a mad dog that threatens a child — a virtue; shooting with the aim of violation or murder — a crime. Outside of these commonplaces the theologians of this order made no promulgations.

In so far as their practical morality is concerned the Jesuits were not at all worse than other monks or Catholic priests, on the contrary, they were superior to them; in any case, more consistent, bolder, and perspicacious. The Jesuits represented a militant organization, strictly centralized, aggressive, and dangerous not only to enemies but also to allies. In his psychology and method of action the Jesuit of the "heroic" period distinguished himself from an average priest as the warrior of a church from its shopkeeper. We have no reason to idealize either one or the other. But it is altogether unworthy to look upon a fanatic warrior with the eyes of an obtuse and slothful shopkeeper.

If we are to remain in the field of purely formal or psychological similitudes, then it can, if you like, be said that the Bolsheviks appear in relation to the democrats and Social Democrats of all hues as did the Jesuits — in relation to the peaceful ecclesiastical hierarchy. Compared to revolutionary Marxists, the Social Democrats and centrists seem like mental defectives, or like a witch doctor alongside a physician: they do not think one problem through to the end, but believe in the power of conjuration and cravenly avoid every difficulty, hoping for a miracle. Opportunists are peaceful shopkeepers in the socialist idea while Bolsheviks are its inveterate warriors. From this comes the hatred and slander against Bolsheviks from those who have an abundance of their historically conditioned faults but not one of their merits.

However, the juxtaposition of Bolshevism and Jesuitism still remains completely one-sided and superficial, of a literary rather than of a historical nature. In accordance with the character and interests of those classes upon which they based themselves, the Jesuits represented reaction, the Protestants — progress. The limitedness of this "progress" in its turn found direct expression in the morality of the Protestants. Thus the teachings of Christ "purified" by them did not at all hinder the city bourgeois Luther from calling for the execution of revolting peasants as "mad dogs." Dr. Martin evidently considered that "the end justifies the means" even before that maxim was attributed to the Jesuits. In turn the Jesuits, competing with Protestantism, adapted themselves ever more to the spirit of bourgeois society, and of the three vows — poverty, chastity, and obedience — they preserved only the third, and at that in an extremely attenuated form. From the point of view of the Christian ideal, the morality of the Jesuits degenerated the more they ceased to be Jesuits. The warriors of the church became its bureaucrats and, like all bureaucrats, adequate enough swindlers.

Jesuitism and utilitarianism

This brief review is sufficient, perhaps, to show what ignorance and narrowness are necessary to consider seriously the contraposition of the "Jesuit" principle "the end justifies the means" to another seemingly higher moral, in which each "means" carries its own moral tag like merchandise with fixed prices in a department store. It is remarkable that the common sense of the Anglo-Saxon philistine has managed to wax indignant at the "Jesuit" principle and simultaneously to find inspiration in the utilitarian morality so characteristic of British philosophy. Yet the criterion of Bentham-John Mill, "the greatest possible happiness of the greatest possible number," signifies that those means are moral which lead to the common welfare as the highest end. In its general philosophical formulations Anglo-Saxon utilitarianism thus fully coincides with the "Jesuit" principle "the end justifies the means." Empiricism, we see, exists in the world only to free us from the necessity of making both ends meet.

Herbert Spencer, into whose empiricism Darwin inculcated the idea of "evolution" as a special vaccine, taught that in the moral sphere evolution proceeds from "sensations" to "ideas." Sensations impose the criterion of immediate pleasure, whereas ideas permit one to be guided by the criterion of *future, lasting, and higher pleasure.* Thus the moral criterion here too is "pleasure" and "happiness." But the content of this criterion acquires breadth and depth depending upon the level of "evolution." In this way Herbert Spencer too, through the methods of his own "evolutionary" utilitarianism, showed that the principle "the end justifies the means" does not embrace anything immoral.

It is naive, however, to expect from this abstract "principle" an answer to the practical question: What may we, and what may we not do? Moreover, the principle the end justifies the means naturally raises the question: And what justifies the end? In practical life as in the historical movement the end and the means constantly change places. A machine under construction is an "end" of production only so that upon entering the factory it may become the "means." Democracy in certain periods is the "end" of the class struggle only so that later it may be transformed into its "means." Not embracing anything immoral, the so-called Jesuit principle fails, however, to resolve the moral problem.

The "evolutionary" utilitarianism of Spencer likewise abandons us halfway without an answer, since, following Darwin, it tries to dissolve the concrete historical morality in the biological needs or in the "social instincts" characteristic of gregarious animals and this at a time when the very understanding of morality arises only in an antagonistic milieu, that is, in a society divided into classes.

Bourgeois evolutionism halts impotently at the threshold of historical society because it does not wish to acknowledge the driving force in the evolution of social forms: *the class struggle.* Morality is one of the ideological functions in this struggle. The ruling class forces *its* ends upon society and habituates it to considering all those means which contradict its ends as immoral. That is the chief function of official morality. It pursues the idea of the "greatest possible happiness" not for the majority but for a small and ever diminishing minority. Such a regime could not have endured for even a week through force alone. It needs the cement of morality. The production of this cement constitutes the profession of the petty-bourgeois theoreticians and moralists. They radiate all the colors of the rainbow but in the final analysis remain apostles of slavery and submission.

"Moral precepts obligatory upon all"

Whoever does not care to return to Moses, Christ, or Mohammed; whoever is not satisfied with eclectic *hodge-podges* must acknowledge that morality is a product of social development; that there is nothing immutable about it; that it serves social interests; that these interests are contradictory; that morality more than any other form of ideology has a class character.

But do not elementary moral precepts exist, worked out in the development of humanity as a whole and indispensable for the existence of every collective body? Undoubtedly such precepts exist but the extent of their action is extremely limited and unstable. Norms "obligatory upon all" become the less forceful the sharper the character assumed by the class struggle. The highest form of the class struggle is civil war, which explodes into midair all moral ties between the hostile classes.

Under "normal" conditions a "normal" person observes the commandment: "Thou shalt not kill!" But if one kills under exceptional conditions for self-defense, the jury acquits that person. If one falls victim to a murderer, the court will kill the murderer. The necessity of courts, as well as that of self-defense, flows from antagonistic interests. In so far as the state is concerned, in peaceful times it limits itself to legalized killings of individuals so that in time of war it may transform the "obligatory" commandment, "Thou shalt not kill!" into its opposite. The most "humane" governments, which in peaceful times "detest" war, proclaim during war that the highest duty of their armies is the extermination of the greatest possible number of people.

The so-called "generally recognized" moral precepts in essence preserve an algebraic, that is, an indeterminate character. They merely express the fact that people in their individual conduct are bound by certain common norms that flow from their being members of society. The highest generalization of these norms is the "categorical imperative" of Kant. But in spite of the fact that it occupies a high position in the philosophic Olympus this imperative does not embody anything categoric because it embodies nothing concrete. It is a shell without content.

This vacuity in the norms obligatory upon all arises from the fact that in all decisive questions people feel their class membership considerably more profoundly and more directly than their membership in "society." The norms of "obligatory" morality are in reality filled with class, that is, antagonistic content. The moral norm becomes the more categoric the less it is "obligatory upon all." The solidarity of workers, especially of strikers or barricade fighters, is incomparably more "categoric" than human solidarity in general.

The bourgeoisie, which far surpasses the proletariat in the completeness and irreconcilability of its class consciousness, is vitally interested in imposing *its* moral philosophy upon the exploited masses. It is exactly for this purpose that the concrete norms of the bourgeois catechism are concealed under moral abstractions patronized by religion, philosophy, or by that hybrid which is called "common sense." The appeal to abstract norms is not a disinterested philosophical mistake but a necessary element in the mechanics of class deception. The exposure of this deceit which retains the tradition of thousands of years is the first duty of a proletarian revolutionist.

The crisis in democratic morality

In order to guarantee the triumph of their interests in big questions, the ruling classes are constrained to make concessions on secondary questions, naturally only so long as these concessions are reconciled in the bookkeeping. During the epoch of capitalist upsurge especially in the last few decades before the World War, these concessions, at least in relation to the top layers of the proletariat, were of a completely genuine nature. Industry at that time expanded almost uninterruptedly. The prosperity of the civilized nations increased — partially, too, that of the toiling masses. Democracy appeared solid. Workers' organizations grew. At the same time reformist tendencies deepened. The relations between the classes softened, at least outwardly. Thus certain elementary moral precepts in social relations were established along with the norms of democracy and the habits of class collaboration. The impression was created of an ever more free, more just, and more humane society. The rising line of progress seemed infinite to "common sense."

Instead, however, war broke out with a train of convulsions, crises, catastrophes, epidemics, and bestiality. The economic life of humankind landed in an impasse. The class antagonisms became sharp and naked. The safety valves of democracy began to explode one after the other. The elementary moral precepts turned out to be even more fragile than the democratic institutions and reformist illusions. Lying, slander, bribery, venality, coercion, murder, grew to unprecedented dimensions. To a stunned simpleton all these vexations seem a temporary result of war. Actually they were and remain manifestations of imperialist decline. The decay of capitalism denotes the decay of contemporary society with its laws and morals.

The "synthesis" of imperialist turpitude is fascism, directly begotten of the bankruptcy of bourgeois democracy confronted with the problems of the imperialist epoch.

Remnants of democracy continue still to exist only in the rich capitalist aristocracies: For each "democrat" in England, France, Holland, Belgium, there is a certain number of colonial slaves; "Sixty Families" dominate the democracy of the United States, and so forth. Moreover, shoots of fascism grow rapidly in all democracies. Stalinism in its turn is the product of imperialist pressure upon a backward and isolated workers' state, a symmetrical complement in its own genre to fascism.

While idealistic philistines — among whom anarchists of course occupy first place — tirelessly unmask Marxist "amoralism" in their press, the American trusts, according to John L. Lewis (CIO), are spending not less than $80,000,000 a year on the practical struggle against revolutionary "demoralization," that is, espionage, bribery of workers, frame-ups, and dark-alley murders. The categorical imperative sometimes chooses circuitous ways for its triumph!

Let us note in justice that the most sincere and at the same time most limited petty-bourgeois moralists still live even today in the idealized memories of yesterday and hope for its return. They do not understand that morality is a function of the class struggle; that democratic morality corresponds to the epoch of liberal and progressive capitalism; that the sharpening of the class struggle in passing through its latest phase definitively and irrevocably destroyed this morality; that in its place came the morality of fascism on one side, on the other the morality of proletarian revolution.

"Common sense"

Democracy and "generally recognized" morality are not the only victims of imperialism. The third suffering martyr is "universal" common sense. This lowest form of the intellect is not only necessary under all conditions but under certain conditions is also adequate. Common sense's basic capital consists of the elementary conclusions of universal experience: not to put one's fingers in fire, whenever possible to proceed along a straight line, not to tease vicious dogs . . . and so forth and so on. Under a stable social milieu common sense is adequate for bargaining, healing, writing articles, leading trade unions, voting in parliament, marrying, and reproducing the race. But when that same common sense attempts to go beyond its valid limits into the arena of more complex generalizations, it is exposed as just a clot of prejudices of a definite class and a definite epoch. A simple capitalist crisis is enough to bring common sense to an impasse; and before such catastrophes as revolution, counterrevolution, and war, common sense proves a perfect fool. In order to understand the catastrophic violations of the "normal" course of events higher qualities of intellect are necessary, and these are philosophically expressed as yet only by dialectical materialism.

Max Eastman, who successfully attempts to endow "common sense" with a most attractive literary style, has fashioned out of the struggle against dialectics nothing less than a profession for himself. Eastman seriously takes the conservative banalities of common sense wedded to good style as "the science of revolution." Supporting the reactionary snobs of *Common Sense,* he expounds to humanity with inimitable assurance that if Trotsky had been guided not by Marxist doctrine but by common sense then he would not . . . have lost power. That inner dialectic which until now has appeared in a succession of determined stages in all revolutions does not exist for Eastman. Reaction's displacing revolution, to him, is determined through insufficient respect for common sense. Eastman does not understand that it is Stalin who in a historical sense fell *victim* to common sense, that is, its inadequacy, since that power which he possesses serves ends hostile to Bolshevism. Marxist doctrine, on the other hand, permitted us to tear away in time from the Thermidorean bureaucracy and continue to serve the ends of international socialism.

Every science, including the "science of revolution," is

verified by experience. Since Eastman well knows how to maintain revolutionary power under the condition of world counterrevolution, then he also knows, we may hope, how to conquer power. It would be very desirable that he finally disclose his secrets. Best of all that it be done in the form of a *draft program for a revolutionary party* under the title: How to Conquer and Hold Power. We fear, however, that it is precisely common sense that will urge Eastman to refrain from such a risky undertaking. And this time common sense will be right.

Marxist doctrine, which Eastman, alas, never understood, permitted us to foresee the inevitability under certain historic conditions of the Soviet Thermidor with all its coils of crimes. That same doctrine long ago predicted the inevitability of the downfall of bourgeois democracy and its morality. Meanwhile, the doctrinaires of "common sense" were caught unaware by fascism and Stalinism. Common sense operates with invariable magnitudes in a world where only change is invariable. Dialectics, on the contrary, takes all phenomena, institutions, and norms in their rise, development, and decay. The dialectical consideration of morals as a subservient and transient product of the class struggle seems to common sense an "amoralism." But there is nothing more stale, narrow, self-satisfied, and cynical than the morals of common sense!

Moralists and the GPU

The Moscow trials provided the occasion for a crusade against Bolshevik "amoralism." However, the crusade was not opened at once. The truth is that in the majority the moralists, directly or indirectly, were friends of the Kremlin. As such they long attempted to hide their amazement and even feigned that nothing unusual had occurred.

But the Moscow trials were not at all an accident. Servile obedience, hypocrisy, the official cult of lying, bribery, and other forms of corruption had already begun to blossom luxuriantly in Moscow by 1924-1925. The future judicial frame-ups were being prepared openly before the eyes of the whole world. There was no lack of warning. The "friends," however, did not wish to notice anything. No wonder: the majority of these gentlemen, in their time irreconcilably hostile to the October Revolution, became friends of the Soviet Union merely according to the degree of its Thermidorean degeneration — the petty-bourgeois democrats of the West recognized in the petty-bourgeois bureaucracy of the East a kindred soul.

Did these people really believe the Moscow accusations? Only the most obtuse. The others did not wish to alarm themselves by verification. Is it reasonable to infringe upon the flattering, comfortable, and often well-paying friendship with the Soviet embassies? Moreover — oh, they did not forget this! — indiscreet truth can injure the prestige of the USSR. These people screened the crimes by utilitarian considerations, that is, openly applied the principle, "the end justifies the means."

The king's counselor Pritt, who succeeded with timeliness in peering under the tunic of the Stalinist Themis and there discovered everything in order, took upon himself the shameless initiative. Romain Rolland, whose moral authority is highly rated by the Soviet publishing house bookkeepers, hastened to issue one of his manifestoes where melancholy lyricism unites with senile cynicism. The French League for the Rights of Man, which thundered about the "amoralism of Lenin and Trotsky" in 1917 when they broke the military alliance with France, hastened to screen Stalin's crimes in 1936 in the interests of the Franco-Soviet pact. A patriotic end justifies, as is known, any means. *The Nation* and *The New Republic* closed their eyes to Yagoda's exploits since their "friendship" with the USSR guaranteed their own authority. Yet only a year ago these gentlemen did not at all declare Stalinism and Trotskyism to be one and the same. They openly stood for Stalin, for his realism, for his justice, and for his Yagoda. They clung to this position as long as they could.

Until the moment of the execution of Tukhachevsky,

Yakir, and the others, the big bourgeoisie of the democratic countries watched the execution of the revolutionists in the USSR, not without pleasure, though feigning abhorrence. In this sense *The Nation* and *The New Republic,* not to speak of Duranty, Louis Fischer, and their kindred prostitutes of the pen, fully responded to the interests of "democratic" imperialism. The execution of the generals alarmed the bourgeoisie, compelling them to understand that the advanced disintegration of the Stalinist apparatus lightened the tasks of Hitler, Mussolini, and the Mikado. The *New York Times* cautiously but insistently began to correct its own Duranty. The Paris *Le Temps* opened its columns slightly to shed light upon the actual situation in the USSR. As for the petty-bourgeois moralists and sycophants, they were never anything but servile echoes of the capitalist class. Moreover, after the International Commission of Inquiry, headed by John Dewey, brought out its verdict, it became clear to every person who thought even a trifle that further open defense of the GPU signified peril of political and moral death. Only at this moment did the "friends" decide to bring the eternal moral truths into God's world, that is, to fall back to the second-line trench.

Frightened Stalinists and semi-Stalinists occupy not the last place among moralists. Eugene Lyons during several years cohabited nicely with the Thermidorean clique, considering himself almost-a-Bolshevik. Withdrawing from the Kremlin—for a reason that is to us a matter of indifference—he rose, of course, immediately into the clouds of idealism. Liston Oak until recently enjoyed such confidence from the Comintern that it entrusted him with conducting its English propaganda for Republican Spain. This did not, naturally, hinder him, once he had relinquished his post, from likewise relinquishing the Marxist alphabet. Expatriate Walter Krivitsky, having broken with the GPU, immediately joined the bourgeois democracy. Evidently this too is the metamorphosis of the very aged Charles Rappoport. Having tossed Stalinism overboard, people of such ilk — they are many — cannot help seeking indemnification in the postulates of abstract morality for the disillusionment and abasement of ideals they have experienced. Ask them: "Why have you switched from the Comintern or GPU ranks to the camp of the bourgeoisie?" They have a ready answer: "Trotskyism is no better than Stalinism."

The disposition of political chessmen

"Trotskyism is revolutionary romanticism; Stalinism — practical politics." Of this banal contraposition with which the average philistine until yesterday justified his friendship with Thermidor against the revolution, there remains not a trace today. Trotskyism and Stalinism are in general no longer counterposed but identified. They are identified, however, only in form not in essence. Having recoiled to the meridian of the "categorical imperative," the democrats actually continue to defend the GPU except with greater camouflage and perfidy. He who slanders the victim aids the executioner. In this case, as in others, morality serves politics.

The democratic philistine and Stalinist bureaucrat are, if not twins, brothers in spirit. In any case they belong politically to the same camp. The present governmental system of France and — if we add the anarchists — of Republican Spain is based on the collaboration of Stalinists, Social Democrats, and liberals. If the British Independent Labour Party appears roughed up it is because for a number of years it has not withdrawn from the embrace of the Comintern. The French Socialist Party expelled the Trotskyists from their ranks exactly when it prepared to fuse with the Stalinists. If the fusion did not materialize, it was not because of principled divergences — what remains of them? — but only because of the fear of the Social Democratic careerists over their posts. Having returned from Spain, Norman Thomas declared that "objectively" the Trotskyists help Franco, and with this subjective absurdity he gave "objective" service to the GPU executioners. This

righteous man expelled the American Trotskyists from
his party precisely as the GPU shot down their cothinkers
in the USSR and in Spain. In many democratic countries,
the Stalinists in spite of their "amoralism" have penetrated
into the government apparatus not without success. In
the trade unions they cohabit nicely with bureaucrats of
other hues. True, the Stalinists have an extremely light-
minded attitude toward the criminal code and in that way
frighten away their "democratic" friends in peaceful times;
but in exceptional circumstances, as indicated by the example of Spain, they more surely become the leaders of the
petty bourgeoisie against the proletariat.

The Second and Amsterdam Internationals naturally
did not take upon themselves the responsibility for the
frame-ups; this work they left to the Comintern. They
themselves kept quiet. Privately they explained that from
a "moral" point of view they were against Stalin, but from
a political point of view — for him. Only when the People's
Front in France cracked irreparably and forced the
Socialists to think about tomorrow did Leon Blum find
at the bottom of his inkwell the necessary formulas for
moral indignation.

If Otto Bauer mildly condemned Vyshinsky's justice,
it was only in order to support Stalin's politics with greater
"impartiality." The fate of socialism, according to Bauer's
recent declaration, is tied with the fate of the Soviet Union.
"And the fate of the Soviet Union," he continues, "is the
fate of Stalinism as long as [!] the inner development of
the Soviet Union itself does not overcome the Stalinist
phase of development." All of Bauer, all of Austro-Marxism, and the full mendacity and rot of Social Democracy
are summed up in this remarkable sentence: "As long as"
the Stalinist bureaucracy is strong enough to murder the
progressive representatives of the "inner development,"
Bauer sticks with Stalin. When in spite of Bauer the revolutionary forces overthrow Stalin, then Bauer will generous-
ly recognize the "inner development" — with not more than
ten years' delay.

Behind the old Internationals, the London Bureau of the centrists trails along, happily combining in itself the characteristics of a kindergarten, a school for mentally arrested adolescents, and a home for invalids. The secretary of the Bureau, Fenner Brockway, began with the declaration that an inquiry into the Moscow trials could "harm the USSR" and proposed instead an investigation into . . . the political activity of Trotsky through an "impartial" commission of five irreconcilable enemies of Trotsky. Brandler and Lovestone publicly solidarized with Yagoda; they retreated only from Yezhov. Jacob Walcher, upon an obviously false pretext, refused to give testimony which was unfavorable to Stalin before the International Commission headed by John Dewey. The putrid morals of these people is only a product of their putrid politics.

But perhaps the most lamentable role is that played by the anarchists. If Stalinism and Trotskyism are one and the same, as they affirm in every sentence, then why do the Spanish anarchists assist the Stalinists in revenging themselves upon the Trotskyists and at the same time upon the revolutionary anarchists? The more frank anarchist theoreticians respond: this is payment for armaments. In other words: the end justifies the means. But what is their *end*? Anarchism? Socialism? No, merely the salvaging of this very same bourgeois democracy which prepared fascism's success. To base ends correspond base means.

That is the real disposition of the figures on the world political board!

Stalinism—a product of the old society

Russia took the greatest leap in history, a leap in which the most progressive forces of the country found their expression. Now in the current reaction, the sweep of which is proportionate to the sweep of the revolution, backwardness is taking its revenge. Stalinism embodies this reaction. The barbarism of old Russian history upon new social bases seems yet more disgusting since it is constrained to conceal itself in hypocrisy unprecedented in history.

The liberals and the Social Democrats of the West, who were constrained by the Russian Revolution into doubt about their rotted ideas, now experienced a fresh influx of courage. The moral gangrene of the Soviet bureaucracy seemed to them the rehabilitation of liberalism. Stereotyped copybooks are drawn out into the light: "Every dictatorship contains the seeds of its own degeneration"; "only democracy guarantees the development of personality"; and so forth. The contrasting of democracy and dictatorship, including in the given case a condemnation of socialism in favor of the bourgeois regime, stuns one from the point of view of theory by its illiterateness and unscrupulousness. The Stalinist pollution, a historical reality, is counterposed to democracy — a suprahistorical abstraction. But democracy also possesses a history in which there is no lack of pollution. In order to characterize Soviet bureaucracy we have borrowed the terms of "Thermidor" and "Bonapartism" from the history of bourgeois democracy because — let this be known to the retarded liberal doctrinaires — *democracy came into the world not at all through the democratic road.* Only a vulgar mentality can satisfy itself by chewing on the theme that Bonapartism was the "natural offspring" of Jacobinism, the historical punishment for infringing upon democracy, and so on. Without the Jacobin retribution upon feudalism, bourgeois democracy would have been absolutely unthinkable. Contrasting the concrete historical stages of Jacobinism, Thermidor, Bonapartism, to the idealized abstraction of "democracy" is as vicious as contrasting the pains of childbirth to a living infant.

Stalinism in turn is not an abstraction of "dictatorship," but an immense bureaucratic reaction against the proletarian dictatorship in a backward and isolated country. The October Revolution abolished privileges, waged war against social inequality, replaced the bureaucracy with self-government of the toilers, abolished secret diplomacy, strove to render all social relationships completely transparent. Stalinism reestablished the most offensive forms of privilege, imbued inequality with a provocative character, strangled mass self-activity under police absolutism, transformed administration into a monopoly of the Kremlin oligarchy, and regenerated the fetishism of power in forms that absolute monarchy dared not dream of.

Social reaction in all forms is constrained to mask its real aims. The sharper the transition from revolution to reaction, the more the reaction is dependent upon the traditions of revolution, that is, the greater its fear of the masses — the more is it forced to resort to mendacity and frame-up in the struggle against the representatives of the revolution. Stalinist frame-ups are not a fruit of Bolshevik "amoralism"; no, like all important events in history, they are a product of the concrete social struggle, and the most perfidious and severest of all at that: the struggle of a new aristocracy against the masses that raised it to power.

Indeed, boundless intellectual and moral obtuseness is required to identify the reactionary police morality of Stalinism with the revolutionary morality of the Bolsheviks. Lenin's party has long ceased to exist — it was shattered between inner difficulties and world imperialism. In its place rose the Stalinist bureaucracy, transmission mechanism of imperialism. The bureaucracy has, on a world scale, replaced class struggle with class collaboration and internationalism with social patriotism. In order to adapt the ruling party to the tasks of reaction, the bureaucracy "renewed" its composition through executing revolutionists and recruiting careerists.

Every reaction regenerates, nourishes, and strengthens those elements of the historic past which the revolution struck but which it could not vanquish. The methods of Stalinism bring to the highest tension, to a culmination and at the same time to an absurdity, all those methods of untruth, brutality, and baseness that constitute the mechanics of control in every class society, including also that of democracy. Stalinism is a single clot of all monstrosities of the historical state, its most malicious caricature and disgusting grimace. When the representatives of old society puritanically counterpose a sterilized democratic abstraction to the gangrene of Stalinism, we can with full justice recommend to them, as to all of old society, that they take a good look at themselves in the warped mirror of Soviet Thermidor. True, the GPU far surpasses all other regimes in the nakedness of its crimes. But this flows from the immense amplitude of events shaking Russia under the influence of world imperialist demoralization.

Morality and revolution

Among the liberals and radicals there are not a few individuals who have assimilated the methods of the materialist interpretation of events and who consider themselves Marxists. This does not hinder them, however, from remaining bourgeois journalists, professors, or politicians. A Bolshevik is inconceivable, of course, without the materialist method, in the sphere of morality as well. But this method serves him not solely for the interpretation of events but rather for the creation of a revolutionary party of the proletariat. It is impossible to accomplish this task without complete independence from the bourgeoisie and their morality. Yet bourgeois public opinion now actually reigns in full sway over the official workers' movement from William Green in the United States, Leon Blum and Maurice Thorez in France, to Garcia Oliver in Spain. In this fact the reactionary character of the present period reaches its sharpest expression.

A revolutionary Marxist cannot begin to approach his historical mission without having broken morally from bourgeois public opinion and its agencies in the proletariat. For this, moral courage of a different calibre is required from that of opening wide one's mouth at meetings and yelling, "Down with Hitler!" "Down with Franco!" It is precisely this resolute, completely thought-out, inflexible rupture of the Bolsheviks from conservative moral philosophy not only of the big but of the petty bourgeoisie that mortally terrorizes democratic phrasemongers, drawing-room prophets, and lobbying heroes. From this derive their complaints about the "amoralism" of the Bolsheviks.

Their identification of bourgeois morals with morals "in general" can best of all, perhaps, be verified at the extreme left wing of the petty bourgeoisie, precisely in the centrist parties of the so-called London Bureau. Since this organization "recognizes" the program of proletarian revolution, our disagreements with it seem, at first glance, secondary. Actually their "recognition" is valueless because it does not bind them to anything. They "recognize" the proletarian revolution as the Kantians recognized the categorical imperative, that is, as a holy principle but not applicable to daily life. In the sphere of practical politics they unite with the worst enemies of the revolution (reformists and Stalinists) for the struggle against us. All their thinking is permeated with duplicity and false-hood. If the centrists, according to a general rule, do not raise themselves to imposing crimes it is only because they forever remain in the byways of politics: they are, so to speak, petty pickpockets of history. For this reason they consider themselves called upon to regenerate the workers' movement with a new morality.

At the extreme left wing of this "left" fraternity stands a small and politically completely insignificant grouping of German emigres who publish the paper *Neuer Weg* (The New Road). Let us bend down lower and listen to these "revolutionary" indicters of Bolshevik amoralism. In a tone of ambiguous pseudopraise the *Neuer Weg* proclaims that the Bolsheviks are distinguished advantageously from other parties by their absence of hypocrisy — they openly declare what others quietly apply in fact, that is, the principle "the end justifies the means." But according to the convictions of *Neuer Weg* such a "bourgeois" precept is incompatible with a "healthy socialist

movement." "Lying and worse are not permissible means
of struggle, as Lenin still considered them." The word
"still" evidently signifies that Lenin did not succeed in
overcoming his delusions only because he failed to live
until the discovery of *The New Road.*

In the formula, "lying and worse," "worse" evidently
signifies violence, murder, and so on, since under equal
conditions violence is worse than lying, and murder —
the most extreme form of violence. We thus come to the
conclusion that lying, violence, murder, are incompatible
with a "healthy socialist movement." What, however, is our
relation to revolution? Civil war is the most severe of
all forms of war. It is unthinkable not only without violence against tertiary figures but, under contemporary
technique, without killing old men, old women, and
children. Must one be reminded of Spain? The only possible
answer of the "friends" of Republican Spain sounds like
this: Civil war is better than fascist slavery. But this completely correct answer merely signifies that the *end* (democracy or socialism) justifies, under certain conditions, such
means as violence and murder. Not to speak about lies!
Without lies war would be as unimaginable as a machine
without oil. In order to safeguard even the session of the
Cortes (February 1, 1938) from fascist bombs, the Bar-
celona government several times deliberately deceived journalists and their own population. Could it have acted
in any other way? Whoever accepts the end: victory over
Franco, must accept the means: civil war with its wake
of horrors and crimes.

Nevertheless, lying and violence "in themselves" warrant
condemnation? Of course, even as does the class society
which generates them. A society without social contradictions will naturally be a society without lies and violence.
However there is no way of building a bridge to that
society save by revolutionary, that is, violent means. The
revolution itself is a product of class society and of
necessity bears its traits. From the point of view of "eternal
truths" revolution is of course "antimoral." But this merely

means that idealist morality is counterrevolutionary, that is, in the service of the exploiters.

"Civil war," the philosopher caught unawares will perhaps respond, "is however a sad exception. But in peaceful times a healthy socialist movement should manage without violence and lying." Such an answer however represents nothing less than a pathetic evasion. There is no impervious demarcation between "peaceful" class struggle and revolution. Every strike embodies in an unexpanded form all the elements of civil war. Each side strives to impress the opponent with an exaggerated picture of its resoluteness to struggle and its material resources. Through their press, agents, and spies the capitalists labor to frighten and demoralize the strikers. From their side, the workers' pickets, where persuasion does not avail, are compelled to resort to force. Thus "lying and worse" are an inseparable part of the class struggle even in its most elementary form. It remains to be added that the very conception of *truth* and *lie* was born of social contradictions.

Revolution and the institution of hostages

Stalin arrests and shoots the children of his opponents after these opponents have been themselves executed under false accusations. With the help of the institution of family hostages Stalin compels those Soviet diplomats to return from abroad who permitted themselves an expression of doubt about the infallibility of Yagoda or Yezhov. The moralists of *Neuer Weg* consider it necessary and timely to remind us on this occasion of the fact that Trotsky in 1919 "also" introduced a law upon hostages. But here it becomes necessary to quote literally: "The detention of innocent relatives by Stalin is disgusting barbarism. But it remains a barbarism as well when it was dictated by Trotsky (1919)." Here is the idealistic moralist in all his beauty! His criteria are as false as the norms of bourgeois democracy — in both cases parity is supposed where in actuality there is not even a trace of it.

We will not insist here upon the fact that the Decree of 1919 led scarcely to even one execution of relatives of those commanders whose perfidy not only caused the loss of innumerable human lives but threatened the revolution with direct annihilation. The question in the end does not concern that. If the revolution had displayed less superfluous generosity from the very beginning, hundreds of thousands of lives would have been saved. Thus or otherwise I carry full responsibility for the Decree of 1919. It was a necessary measure in the struggle against the oppressors. Only in the historical content of the struggle lies the justification of the decree as in general the justification of the whole civil war which, too, can be called, not without foundation, "disgusting barbarism."

We leave to some Emil Ludwig or his ilk the drawing of Abraham Lincoln's portrait with rosy little wings. Lincoln's significance lies in his not hesitating before the most severe means, once they were found to be necessary, in achieving a great historic aim posed by the development of a young nation. The question lies not even in which of the warring camps caused or itself suffered the greatest number of victims. History has different yardsticks for the cruelty of the Northerners and the cruelty of the Southerners in the Civil War. A slaveholder who through cunning and violence shackles a slave in chains, and a slave who through cunning and violence breaks the chains — let not the contemptible eunuchs tell us that they are equals before a court of morality!

After the Paris Commune had been drowned in blood and the reactionary knaves of the whole world dragged its banner in the filth of vilification and slander, there were not a few democratic philistines who, adapting themselves to reaction, slandered the Communards for shooting sixty-four hostages headed by the Paris archbishop. Marx did not hesitate a moment in defending this bloody act of the Commune. In a circular issued by the General

Council of the First International, which seethes with the fiery eruption of lava, Marx first reminds us of the bourgeoisie adopting the institution of hostages in the struggle against both colonial peoples and their own toiling masses and afterward refers to the systematic execution of the Commune captives by the frenzied reactionaries, continuing: ". . . the Commune, to protect their [the captives'] lives, was obliged to resort to the Prussian practice of securing hostages. The lives of the hostages had been forfeited over and over again by the continued shooting of prisoners on the part of the Versaillese. How could they be spared any longer after the carnage with which MacMahon's praetorians celebrated their entry into Paris? Was even the last check upon the unscrupulous ferocity of bourgeois governments — the taking of hostages — to be made a mere sham of?" Thus Marx defended the execution of hostages although behind his back in the General Council sat not a few Fenner Brockways, Norman Thomases and other Otto Bauers. But so fresh was the indignation of the world proletariat against the ferocity of the Versaillese that the reactionary moralistic bunglers preferred to keep silent in expectation of times more favorable to them which, alas, were not slow in appearing. Only after the definite triumph of reaction did the petty-bourgeois moralists, together with the trade union bureaucrats and the anarchist phrasemongers, destroy the First International.

When the October Revolution was defending itself against the united forces of imperialism on a 5,000-mile front, the workers of the whole world followed the course of the struggle with such ardent sympathy that in their forums it was extremely risky to indict the "disgusting barbarism" of the institution of hostages. Complete degeneration of the Soviet state and the triumph of reaction in a number of countries was necessary before the moralists crawled out of their crevices . . . to aid Stalin. If it is true that the repressions safeguarding the privileges of the new aristocracy have the same moral value as the revolutionary measures of the liberating struggle, then Stalin is completely justified, if . . . if the proletarian revolution is not completely condemned.

Seeking examples of immorality in the events of the Russian civil war, Messrs. Moralists find themselves at the came time constrained to close their eyes to the fact that the Spanish revolution also produced an institution of hostages, at least during that period when it was a genuine revolution of the masses. If the indicters dare not attack the Spanish workers for their "disgusting barbarism," it is only because the ground of the Pyrennean peninsula is still too hot for them. It is considerably more convenient to return to 1919. This is already history, the old men have forgotten and the young ones have not yet learned. For the same reason pharisees of various hues return to Kronstadt and Makhno with such obstinacy — here exists a free outlet for moral effluvia!

"Morality of the Kaffirs"

It is impossible not to agree with the moralists that history chooses cruel pathways. But what type of conclusion for practical activity is to be drawn from this? Leo Tolstoy recommended that we ignore the social conventions and perfect ourselves. Mahatma Gandhi advises that we drink goat's milk. Alas, the "revolutionary" moralists of *Neuer Weg* did not drift far from these recipes. "We should free ourselves," they preach, "from those morals of the Kaffirs to whom only what the enemy does is wrong." Excellent advice! "We should free ourselves. . . ." Tolstoy recommended in addition that we free ourselves from the sins of the flesh. However, statistics fail to confirm the success of his recommendation. Our centrist homunculi have succeeded in elevating themselves to supraclass morality in a class society. But almost 2,000 years have passed since it was stated: "Love your enemies," "Offer also the other cheek. . . ." However, even the holy Roman father so far has not "freed himself" from hatred against his enemies. Truly, Satan, the enemy of mankind, is powerful!

To apply different criteria to the actions of the exploiters and the exploited signifies, according to these pitiful homunculi, standing on the level of the "morals of the Kaffirs." First of all such a contemptuous reference to the Kaffirs is hardly proper from the pen of "socialists." Are the morals of the Kaffirs really so bad? Here is what the *Encyclopaedia Britannica* says upon the subject:

"In their social and political relations they display great tact and intelligence; they are remarkably brave, warlike, and hospitable, and were honest and truthful until through contact with the whites they became suspicious, revengeful, and thievish, besides acquiring most European vices." It is impossible not to arrive at the conclusion that white missionaries, preachers of eternal morals, participated in the corruption of the Kaffirs.

If we should tell the toiler-Kaffir how the workers arose in a part of our planet and caught their exploiters unawares, he would be very pleased. On the other hand, he would be chagrined to discover that the oppressors had succeeded in deceiving the oppressed. A Kaffir who has not been demoralized by missionaries to the marrow of his bones will never apply the same abstract moral norms to the oppressors and the oppressed. Yet he will easily comprehend an explanation that it is the function of these abstract norms to prevent the oppressed from arising against their oppressors.

What an instructive coincidence! In order to slander the Bolsheviks, the missionaries of *Neuer Weg* were compelled at the same time to slander the Kaffirs; moreover in both cases the slander follows the line of the official bourgeois lie: against revolutionists and against the colored races. No, we prefer the Kaffirs to all missionaries, both spiritual and secular!

It is not necessary in any case, however, to overestimate the conscientiousness of the moralists of *The New Road* and other blind alleys. The intentions of these people are not so bad. But despite these intentions they serve as levers in the mechanics of reaction. In such a period as the present when the petty-bourgeois parties who cling to the liberal bourgeois or its shadow (the politics of the "People's Front") paralyze the proletariat and pave the road for fascism (Spain, France . . .), the Bolsheviks, that is, revolutionary Marxists, become especially odious figures in the eyes of bourgeois public opinion. The fundamental political pressure of our time shifts from right to left. In the final analysis the whole weight of reaction bears down upon the shoulders of a tiny revolutionary minority. This minority is called the Fourth International. *Voila l'ennemi!* There is the enemy!

In the mechanics of reaction Stalinism occupies many leading positions. All groupings of bourgeois society, including the anarchists, utilize its aid in the struggle against the proletarian revolution. At the same time the petty-bourgeois democrats attempt, at least to the extent of fifty percent, to cast the repulsiveness of the crimes of its Moscow ally upon the indomitable revolutionary minority. Herein lies the sense of the now stylish dictum: "Trotskyism and Stalinism are one and the same." The adversaries of the Bolsheviks and the Kaffirs thus aid reaction in slandering the party of revolution.

The "amoralism" of Lenin

The Russian Social Revolutionaries were always the most moral individuals: essentially they were composed of ethics alone. This did not prevent them, however, at the time of revolution from deceiving the Russian peasants. In the Parisian organ of Kerensky, that very ethical socialist who was the forerunner of Stalin in manufacturing spurious accusations against the Bolsheviks, another old Social Revolutionary, Zenzinov, writes: "Lenin, as is known, taught that for the sake of gaining the desired ends communists can, and sometimes must 'resort to all sorts of devices, maneuvers and subterfuge' . . ." (*New Russia,* February 17, 1938, p. 3). From this they draw the ritualistic conclusion: Stalinism is the natural offspring of Leninism.

Unfortunately, the ethical indicter is not even capable of quoting honestly. Lenin said: "It is necessary to be able . . . to resort to all sorts of devices, maneuvers, and illegal methods, to evasion and subterfuge, *in order to penetrate into the trade unions, to remain in them, and to carry on communist work in them at all costs."* The necessity for evasion and maneuvers, according to Lenin's explanation, is called forth by the fact that the reformist bureaucracy, betraying the workers to capital, baits revolutionists, persecutes them, and even resorts to turning the bourgeois police upon them. "Maneuvers" and "subterfuge" are in this case only methods of valid self-defense against the perfidious reformist bureaucracy.

The party of this very Zenzinov once carried on illegal work against czarism, and later — against the Bolsheviks. In both cases it resorted to craftiness, evasion, false passports, and other forms of "subterfuge." All these *means* were considered not only "ethical" but also heroic because they corresponded to the political *aims* of the petty bourgeoisie. But the situation changes at once when proletarian revolutionists are forced to resort to conspirative measures against the petty-bourgeois democracy. The key to the morality of these gentlemen has, as we see, a class character!

The "amoralist" Lenin openly, in the press, gives advice concerning military craftiness against perfidious leaders. And the moralist Zenzinov maliciously chops both ends from the quotation in order to deceive the reader — the ethical indicter is proved as usual a petty swindler. Not for nothing was Lenin fond of repeating: It is very difficult to meet a conscientious adversary!

A worker who does not conceal the "truth" about the strikers' plans from the capitalists is simply a betrayer deserving contempt and boycott. The soldier who discloses the "truth" to the enemy is punished as a spy. Kerensky tried to lay at the Bolsheviks' door the accusation of having disclosed the "truth" to Ludendorff's staff. It appears that even the "holy truth" is not an end in itself.

More imperious criteria which, as analysis demonstrates, carry a class character, rule over it.

The life-and-death struggle is unthinkable without military craftiness, in other words, without lying and deceit. May the German proletariat then not deceive Hitler's police? Or perhaps Soviet Bolsheviks have an "immoral" attitude when they deceive the GPU? Every pious bourgeois applauds the cleverness of police who succeed through craftiness in seizing a dangerous gangster. Is military craftiness really impermissible when the question concerns the overthrow of the gangsters of imperialism?

Norman Thomas speaks about "that strange communist amorality in which nothing matters but the party and its power" (*Socialist Call*, March 12, 1938, p. 5). Moreover, Thomas throws into one heap the present Comintern, that is, the conspiracy of the Kremlin bureaucracy against the working class, with the Bolshevik Party, which represented a conspiracy of the advanced workers against the bourgeoisie. This thoroughly dishonest juxtaposition has already been sufficiently exposed above. Stalinism merely screens itself under the cult of the party; actually it destroys and tramples the party in filth. It is true, however, that to a Bolshevik the party is everything. The drawing-room socialist Thomas is surprised by and rejects a similar relationship between a revolutionist and revolution because he himself is only a bourgeois with a socialist "ideal." In the eyes of Thomas and his kind the party is only a secondary instrument for electoral combinations and other similar uses, not more. His personal life, interests, ties, moral criteria exist outside the party. With hostile astonishment he looks down upon the Bolshevik to whom the party is a weapon for the revolutionary reconstruction of society, including also its morality. To a revolutionary Marxist there can be no contradiction between personal morality and the interests of the party, since the party embodies in his consciousness the very highest tasks and aims of humanity. It is naive to imagine that Thomas has a higher understanding of morality than the Marxists. He merely has a base conception of the party.

"All that arises is worthy of perishing," says the dialectician Goethe. The perishing of the Bolshevik Party — an episode in world reaction — does not, however, disparage its worldwide historic significance. In the period of its revolutionary ascendance, that is, when it actually represented the proletarian vanguard, it was the most honest party in history. Wherever it could, of course, it deceived the class enemies; on the other hand it told the toilers the truth, the whole truth, and nothing but the truth. Only thanks to this did it succeed in winning their trust to a degree never before achieved by any other party in the world.

The clerks of the ruling classes call the organizers of this party "amoralists." In the eyes of conscious workers this accusation carries a complimentary character. It signifies: Lenin refused to recognize moral norms established by slave-owners for their slaves and never observed by the slave-owners themselves; he called upon the proletariat to extend the class struggle into the moral sphere too. Whoever fawns before precepts established by the enemy will never vanquish that enemy!

The "amoralism" of Lenin, that is, his rejection of supra-class morals, did not hinder him from remaining faithful to one and the same ideal throughout his whole life; from devoting his whole being to the cause of the oppressed; from displaying the highest conscientiousness in the sphere of ideas and the highest fearlessness in the sphere of action; from maintaining an attitude untainted by the least superiority to an "ordinary" worker, to a defenseless woman, to a child. Does it not seem that "amoralism" in the given case is only a pseudonym for higher human morality?

An instructive episode

Here it is proper to relate an episode which, in spite of its modest dimensions, does not badly illustrate the difference between *their* morals and *ours*. In 1935, through a letter to my Belgian friends, I developed the conception that the attempt of a young revolutionary party to organize "its own" trade unions is equivalent to suicide. It is necessary to find the workers where they are. But this means paying dues in order to sustain an opportunist apparatus? "Of course," I replied, "for the right to undermine the reformists it is necessary temporarily to pay them a contribution." But reformists will not permit us to undermine them? "True," I answered, "undermining demands conspirative measures. Reformists are the political police of the bourgeoisie within the working class. We must act without their permission, and against their interdiction. . . ." Through an accidental raid on Comrade D.'s home in connection, if I am not mistaken, with the matter of supplying arms for the Spanish workers, the Belgian police seized my letter. Within several days it was published. The press of Vandervelde, de Man, and Spaak did not of course spare lightning against my "Machiavellianism" and "Jesuitism." And who are these accusers? Vandervelde, president for many years of the Second International, long ago became a trusted servant of Belgian capital. de Man, who in a series of ponderous tomes ennobled socialism with idealistic morals, making overtures to religion, seized the first suitable occasion in which to betray the workers and become a common bourgeois minister. Even more lovely is Spaak's case. A year and a half previously this gentleman belonged to the left-socialist opposition and came to me in France for advice upon the methods of struggle against Vandervelde's bureaucracy. I set forth the same conceptions which later constituted my letter. But within a year after his visit, Spaak rejected the thorns for the roses. Betraying his comrades of the opposition, he became one of the most cynical ministers of Belgian capital. In the trade unions and in their own party these gentlemen stifle every critical voice, systematically corrupt and bribe the most advanced workers and just as systematically expel the refractory ones. They are distinguished from the GPU only by the fact that they have not yet resorted to spilling blood — as good patriots they husband the workers' blood for the next imperialist war. Obviously — one must be a most hellish abomination, a moral deformation, a "Kaffir," a Bolshevik, in order to advise the revolutionary workers to observe the precepts of conspiracy in the struggle against these gentlemen!

From the point of view of the Belgian laws, my letter did not of course contain anything criminal. The duty of the "democratic" police was to return the letter to the addressee with an apology. The duty of the Socialist Party was to protest against the raid which had been dictated by concern over General Franco's interests. But Messrs. Socialists were not at all shy at utilizing the indecent police service — without this they could not have enjoyed the happy occasion of once more exposing the superiority of their morals over the amoralism of the Bolsheviks.

Everything is symbolic in this episode. The Belgian Social Democrats dumped the buckets of their indignation upon me exactly while their Norwegian cothinkers held me and my wife under lock and key in order to prevent us from defending ourselves against the accusations of the GPU. The Norwegian government well knew that the Moscow accusations were spurious — the Social Democratic semiofficial newspaper affirmed this openly during the first days. But Moscow touched the Norwegian shipowners and fish merchants on the pocketbook — and Messrs. Social Democrats immediately flopped down on all fours. The leader of the party, Martin Tranmael, is not only an authority in the moral sphere but openly a righteous person: he does not drink, does not smoke, does not indulge in meat, and in winter bathes in an ice-hole. This did not hinder him, after he had arrested us upon the order of the GPU, from especially inviting a Norwegian agent of the GPU, one Jacob Fries — a bourgeois without honor or conscience — to calumniate me. But enough. . . .

The morals of these gentlemen consist of conventional precepts and turns of speech, which are supposed to screen their interests, appetites, and fears. In the majority they are ready for any baseness — rejection of convictions, perfidy, betrayal — in the name of ambition or cupidity. In the holy sphere of personal interests the end to them justifies any means. But it is precisely because of this that they require special codes of morals, durable, and at the same time elastic, like good suspenders. They detest anyone who exposes their professional secrets to the masses. In "peaceful" times their hatred is expressed in slander — in Billingsgate or "philosophical" language. In times of sharp social conflicts, as in Spain, these moralists, hand in hand with the GPU, murder revolutionists. In order to justify themselves, they repeat: "Trotskyism and Stalinism are one and the same."

Dialectical interdependence of end and means

A means can be justified only by its end. But the end in its turn needs to be justified. From the Marxist point of view, which expresses the historical interests of the proletariat, the end is justified if it leads to increasing the power of humanity over nature and to the abolition of the power of one person over another.

"We are to understand then that in achieving this end anything is permissible?" demands the philistine sarcastically, demonstrating that he understood nothing. That is permissible, we answer, which *really* leads to the liberation of humanity. Since this end can be achieved only through revolution, the liberating morality of the proletariat of necessity is endowed with a revolutionary character. It irreconcilably counteracts not only religious dogma but all kinds of idealistic fetishes, these philosophic gendarmes of the ruling class. It deduces a rule for conduct from the laws of the development of society, thus primarily from the class struggle, this law of all laws.

"Just the same," the moralist continues to insist, "does it mean that in the class struggle against capitalists all means are permissible: lying, frame-up, betrayal, murder, and so on?" Permissible and obligatory are those and only those means, we answer, which unite the revolutionary proletariat, fill their hearts with irreconcilable hostility to oppression, teach them contempt for official morality and its democratic echoers, imbue them with consciousness of their own historic mission, raise their courage and spirit of self-sacrifice in the struggle. Precisely from this it flows that *not* all means are permissible. When we say that the end justifies the means, then for us the conclusion follows that the great revolutionary end spurns those base means and w.ays which set one part of the working class against other parts, or attempt to make the masses happy without their participation; or lower the faith of the masses in themselves and their organization, replacing it by worship for the "leaders." Primarily and irreconcilably, revolutionary morality rejects servility in relation to the bourgeoisie and haughtiness in relation to the toilers, that is, those characteristics in which petty-bourgeois pedants and moralists are thoroughly steeped.

These criteria do not, of course, give a ready answer to the question as to what is permissible and what is not permissible in each separate case. There can be no such automatic answers. Problems of revolutionary morality are fused with the problems of revolutionary strategy and tactics. The living experience of the movement under the clarification of theory provides the correct answer to these problems.

Dialectical materialism does not know dualism between means and end. The end flows naturally from the historical movement. Organically the means are subordinated to the end. The immediate end becomes the means for a further end. In his play *Franz von Sickingen,* Ferdinand Lassalle puts the following words into the mouth of one of the heroes:

Do not only show the goal, show the path as well.

For so closely interwoven with one another are path
  and goal
That a change in one means a change in the other,
And a different path gives rise to a different goal.

Lassalle's lines are not at all perfect. Still worse is the
fact that in practical politics Lassalle himself diverged
from the above expressed precept — it is sufficient to recall
that he went as far as secret agreements with Bismarck!
But the dialectical interdependence between means and
end is expressed entirely correctly in the above-quoted
sentences. Seeds of wheat must be sown in order to yield
an ear of wheat.
Is individual terror, for example, permissible or impermissible from the point of view of "pure morals"? In
this abstract form the question does not exist at all for
us. Conservative Swiss bourgeois even now render official
praise to the terrorist William Tell. Our sympathies are
fully on the side of Irish, Russian, Polish, or Hindu terror-
ists in their struggle against national and political oppression. The assassinated Kirov, a rude satrap, does
not call forth any sympathy. Our relation to the assassin
remains neutral only because we know not what motives
guided him. If it became known that Nikolaev acted as
a conscious avenger for workers' rights trampled upon
by Kirov, our sympathies would be fully on the side
of the assassin. However, not the question of subjective
motives but that of objective efficacy has for us the decisive significance. Are the given means really capable
of leading to the goal? In relation to individual terror,
both theory and experience bear witness that such is
not the case. To the terrorist we say: It is impossible
to replace the masses; only in the mass movement can
you find effective expression for your heroism. However,
under conditions of civil war, the assassination of individual oppressors ceases to be an act of individual
terror. If, we shall say, a revolutionist bombed General

Franco and his staff into the air, it would hardly evoke moral indignation even from the democratic eunuchs. Under the conditions of civil war a similar act would be politically completely effective. Thus, even in the sharpest question — murder of man by man — moral absolutes prove futile. Moral evaluations, along with political ones, flow from the inner needs of struggle.

The liberation of the workers can come only through the workers themselves. There is, therefore, no greater crime than deceiving the masses, palming off defeats as victories, friends as enemies, bribing workers' leaders, fabricating legends, staging false trials, in a word, doing what the Stalinists do. These means can serve only one end: lengthening the domination of a clique already condemned by history. But they cannot serve to liberate the masses. That is why the Fourth International wages a life and death struggle against Stalinism.

The masses, of course, are not at all impeccable. Idealization of the masses is foreign to us. We have seen them under different conditions, at different stages and in addition in the biggest political shocks. We have observed their strong and weak sides. Their strong side — resoluteness, self-sacrifice, heroism — has always found its clearest expression in times of revolutionary upsurge. During this period the Bolsheviks headed the masses. Afterward a different historical chapter loomed when the weak side of the oppressed came to the forefront: heterogeneity, insufficiency of culture, narrowness of world outlook. The masses tired of the tension, became disillusioned, lost faith in themselves — and cleared the road for the new aristocracy. In this epoch the Bolsheviks ("Trotskyists") found themselves isolated from the masses. Practically speaking, we went through two such big historic cycles: 1897-1905, years of flood tide; 1907-1913, years of the ebb; 1917-1923, a period of upsurge unprecedented in history; finally, a new period of reaction, which has not ended even today. In these immense events the "Trotskyists" learned the rhythm of history, that is, the dialectics of the class struggle. They also learned, it seems, and to a certain degree successfully, how to subordinate their subjective plans and programs to this objective rhythm. They learned not to fall into despair over the fact that the laws of history do not depend upon their individual tastes and are not subordinated to their own moral criteria. They learned to subordinate their individual tastes to the laws of history. They learned not to become frightened by the most powerful enemies if their power is in contradiction to the needs of historical development. They know how to swim against the stream in the deep conviction that the new historic flood will carry them to the other shore. Not all will reach that shore, many will drown. But to participate in this movement with open eyes and with an intense will — only this can give the highest moral satisfaction to a thinking being!

Coyoacan, February 16, 1938

P. S. — I wrote these lines during those days when my son struggled, unknown to me, with death. I dedicate to his memory this small work which, I hope, would have met with his approval — Leon Sedov was a genuine revolutionist and despised the pharisees.

The Moralists and Sycophants against Marxism
by Leon Trotsky

Peddlers of indulgences and their socialist allies, or the cuckoo in a strange nest

The pamphlet *Their Morals and Ours* possesses merit at least in this, that it has compelled certain philistines and sycophants to expose themselves completely. The first clippings from the French and Belgian press received by me testify to this. The most intelligible of its kind is the review which appeared in the Parisian Catholic newspaper *La Croix*. These gentlemen have a system of their own, and they are not ashamed to defend it. They stand for absolute morality, and above all for the butcher Franco. It is the will of God. Behind them stands a Heavenly Sanitarian who gathers and cleans all the filth in their wake. It is hardly surprising that they should condemn as unworthy the morality of revolutionists who assume responsibility for themselves. But we are now interested not in professional peddlers of indulgences but in moralists who manage to do without God while seeking to put themselves in His stead.

The Brussels "socialist" newspaper *Le Peuple*—here is virtue's hideout! —has been able to find nothing in our little book except a criminal recipe for building secret cells in the pursuit of the most immoral of all goals, that of undermining the prestige and revenues of the Belgian labor bureaucracy. It may of course be said in reply that this bureaucracy is smeared with countless betrayals and sheer swindles (we need only recall the history of the "Labor Bank"!); that it stifles every glimmer of critical thought in the working class; that in its practical morality it is in no way superior to its political ally, the Catholic hierarchy. But, in the first place, only very poorly educated people would mention such unpleasant things; secondly, all these gentlemen, whatever their petty sins, keep in reserve the highest principles of morality. To this Henri de Man sees personally, and before his high authority we Bolsheviks cannot of course expect any indulgence.

Before passing on to other moralists, let us pause for a moment on a prospectus issued by the French publishers of our little book.* By its very nature, a prospectus either recommends a book, or, at least, delineates objectively its contents. We have before us a prospectus of an entirely different type. Suffice it to adduce only one example: "Trotsky is of the opinion that his party, once in power and now in opposition, has always represented the genuine proletariat, and he himself—genuine morality. From this he concludes for instance the following: Shooting of hostages assumes an entirely different meaning depending upon whether the order is issued by Stalin or Trotsky. . . ." This quotation is quite ample for an appraisal of the behind-the-scenes commentator. It is the unquestionable right of an author to supervise a prospectus. But inasmuch as in the present case the author happens to be on the other side of the ocean, some "friend," apparently profiting from the publisher's lack of information, contrived to slip into a strange nest and deposit there his little egg—oh! it is of course a very tiny egg, an almost virginal egg. Who is the author of this prospectus? Victor Serge, who translated the book and who is at the same time its severest critic, can easily supply the information. I should not be surprised if it turned out that the prospectus was written . . . naturally, not by Victor Serge but by one of his disciples who imitates both his master's ideas and his style. But, maybe after all, it is the master himself, that is, Victor Serge in his capacity of "friend" of the author?

* See Appendix One.

"Hottentot morality"!

Souvarine and other sycophants have of course immediately seized upon the foregoing statement in the prospectus which saves them the bother of casting about for poisoned sophisms. If Trotsky takes hostages, it is good; if Stalin, it is bad. In the face of such "Hottentot morality," it is not difficult to give vent to noble indignation. Yet there is nothing easier than to expose on the basis of this most recent example the hollowness and falsity of this indignation. Victor Serge publicly became a member of the POUM, a Catalan party which had its own militia at the front during the civil war. At the front, as is well known, people shoot and kill. It may therefore be said: "For Victor Serge killings assume entirely different meaning depending upon whether the order is issued by General Franco or by the leaders of Victor Serge's own party." If our moralist had tried to think out the meaning of his own actions before trying to instruct others, he would in all probability have said the following: But the Spanish workers fought to emancipate the people while Franco's gangs fought to reduce it to slavery! Serge will not be able to invent a different answer. In other words, he will have to repeat the "Hottentot"* argument of Trotsky in relation to the hostages.

Once again on hostages

However, it is possible and even probable that our moralists will refuse to say candidly that which is, and will attempt to beat about the bush: "To kill at the front is one thing, to shoot hostages is something else again!" This argument, as we shall shortly prove, is simply stupid. But let us stop for a moment on the ground chosen by

* We shall not dwell here on the shabby custom of referring contemptuously to the Hottentots in order thereby more radiantly to represent the morality of the white slaveholders. It was adequately dealt with in the pamphlet [*Their Morals and Ours,* p. 41]. — L. T.

our adversary. The system of hostages, you say, is immoral "in itself"? Good, that is what we want to know. But this system has been practiced in all the civil wars of ancient and modern history. It obviously flows from the nature of civil war itself. From this it is possible to draw only one conclusion, namely, that the very nature of civil war is immoral. That is the standpoint of the newspaper *La Croix,* which holds that it is necessary to obey the powers-that-be, for power emanates from God. And Victor Serge? He has no considered point of view. To drop a little egg in a strange nest is one thing, to define one's position on complex historical problems is something else again. I readily admit that people of such transcendent morality as Azana, Caballero, Negrin and Co. were against taking hostages from the fascist camp: On both sides you have bourgeois, bound by family and material ties and convinced that even in case of defeat they would not only save themselves but would retain their beefsteaks. In their own fashion, they were right. But the fascists did take hostages among the proletarian revolutionists, and the proletarians, on their part, took hostages from among the fascist bourgeoisie, for they knew the menace that a defeat, even partial and temporary, implied for them and their class brothers.

Victor Serge himself cannot tell exactly what he wants: whether to purge the civil war of the practice of hostages, or to purge human history of civil war? The petty-bourgeois moralist thinks episodically, in fragments, in clumps, being incapable of approaching phenomena in their internal connection. Artificially set apart, the question of hostages is for him a particular moral problem, independent of those general conditions which engender armed conflicts between classes. Civil war is the supreme expression of the class struggle. To attempt to subordinate it to abstract "norms" means in fact to disarm the workers in the face of an enemy armed to the teeth. The petty-bourgeois moralist is the younger brother of the bourgeois pacifist who wants to "humanize" warfare by prohibiting the use of poison gases, the bombardment of unfortified cities, etc. Politically, such programs serve only to deflect the thoughts of the people from revolution as the only method of putting an end to war.

The dread of bourgeois public opinion

Entangled in his contradictions, the moralist might perhaps try to argue that an "open" and "conscious" struggle between two camps is one thing, but the seizure of non-participants in the struggle is something else again. This argument, however, is only a wretched and stupid evasion. In Franco's camp fought tens of thousands who were duped and conscripted by force. The Republican armies shot at and killed these unfortunate captives of a reactionary general. Was this moral or immoral? Furthermore, modern warfare, with its long-range artillery, aviation, poison gases, and finally, with its train of devastation, famine, fires, and epidemics, inevitably involves the loss of hundreds of thousands and millions, the aged and the children included, who do not participate directly in the struggle. People taken as hostages are at least bound by ties of class and family solidarity with one of the camps, or with the leaders of that camp. A conscious selection is possible in taking hostages. A projectile fired from a gun or dropped from a plane is let loose by hazard and may easily destroy not only foes but friends, or their parents and children. Why then do our moralists set apart the question of hostages and shut their eyes to the entire content of civil war? Because they are not too courageous. As "leftists" they fear to break openly with revolution. As petty bourgeois they dread destroying the bridges to official public opinion. In condemning the system of hostages they feel themselves in good company — against the Bolsheviks. They maintain a cowardly silence about Spain. Against the fact that the Spanish workers, anarchists, and POUMists took hostages, V. Serge will protest . . . in twenty years.

The moral code of civil war

To the very same category pertains still another of V. Serge's discoveries, namely, that the degeneration of the Bolsheviks dates from the moment when the Cheka was given the right of deciding behind closed doors the fate of people. Serge plays with the concept of revolution, writes poems about it, but is incapable of understanding it as it is.

Public trials are possible only in conditions of a stable regime. Civil war is a condition of the extreme instability of society and the state. Just as it is impossible to publish in newspapers the plans of the general staff, so is it impossible to reveal in public trials the conditions and circumstances of conspiracies, for the latter are intimately linked with the course of the civil war. Secret trials, beyond a doubt, greatly increase the possibility of mistakes. This merely signifies, and we concede it readily, that the circumstances of civil war are hardly favorable for the exercise of impartial justice. And what more than that?

We propose that V. Serge be appointed as chairman of a commission composed of, say, Marceau Pivert, Souvarine, Waldo Frank, Max Eastman, Magdeleine Paz and others to draft a moral code for civil warfare. Its general character is clear in advance. Both sides pledge not to take hostages. Public trials remain in force. For their proper functioning, complete freedom of the press is preserved throughout the civil war. Bombardment of cities, being detrimental to public justice, freedom of the press, and the inviolability of the individual, is strictly prohibited. For similar and sundry other reasons the use of artillery is outlawed. And inasmuch as rifles, hand grenades, and even bayonets unquestionably exercise a baleful influence upon human beings as well as upon democracy in general, the use of weapons, firearms or sidearms, in the civil war is strictly forbidden.

Marvelous code! Magnificent monument to the rhetoric of Victor Serge and Magdeleine Paz! However, so long as this code remains unaccepted as a rule of conduct by all the oppressors and the oppressed, the warring classes will seek to gain victory *by every means,* while petty-bourgeois moralists will continue as heretofore to wander in confusion between the two camps. Subjectively, they sympathize with the oppressed — no one doubts that. Objectively, they remain captives of the morality of the ruling class and seek to impose it upon the oppressed instead of helping them elaborate the morality of insurrection.

The masses have nothing at all to do with it!

Victor Serge has disclosed in passing what caused the collapse of the Bolshevik Party: excessive centralism, mistrust of ideological struggle, lack of freedom-loving (*"libertaire,"* in reality anarchist) spirit. More confidence in the masses, more freedom! All this is outside time and space. But the masses are by no means identical: there are revolutionary masses, there are passive masses, there are reactionary masses. The very same masses are at different times inspired by different moods and objectives. It is just for this reason that a centralized organization of the vanguard is indispensable. Only a party, wielding the authority it has won, is capable of overcoming the vacillation of the masses themselves. To invest the mass with traits of sanctity and to reduce one's program to amorphous "democracy," is to dissolve oneself in the class as it is, to turn from a vanguard into a rearguard, and by this very thing, to renounce revolutionary tasks. On the other hand, if the dictatorship of the proletariat means anything at all, then it means that the vanguard of the class is armed with the resources of the state in order to repel dangers, including those emanating from the backward layers of the proletariat itself. All this is elementary; all this has been demonstrated by the experience of Russia, and confirmed by the experience of Spain.

But the whole secret is this, that demanding freedom "for the masses," Victor Serge in reality demands freedom for himself and for his compeers, freedom from all control, all discipline, even, if possible, from all criticism. The "masses" have nothing at all to do with it. When our "democrat" scurries from right to left, and from left to right, sowing confusion and skepticism, he imagines it to be the realization of a salutary freedom of thought. But when we evaluate from the Marxist standpoint the vacillations of a disillusioned petty-bourgeois intellectual, that seems to him an assault upon his individuality. He then enters into an alliance with all the confusionists for a crusade against our despotism and our sectarianism.

The internal democracy of a revolutionary party is not a goal in itself. It must be supplemented and bounded by centralism. For a Marxist the question has always been: democracy for what? For which program? The framework of the program is at the same time the framework of democracy. Victor Serge demanded of the Fourth International that it give freedom of action to all confusionists, sectarians, and centrists of the POUM, Vereecken, Marceau Pivert types, to conservative bureaucrats of the Sneevliet type or mere adventurers of the R. Molinier type. On the other hand, Victor Serge has systematically helped centrist organizations drive from their ranks the partisans of the Fourth International. We are very well acquainted with that democratism: it is compliant, accommodating, and conciliatory — *towards the right*; at the same time it is exigent, malevolent, and tricky — *towards the left.* It merely represents the regime of self-defense of petty-bourgeois centrism.

The struggle against Marxism

If Victor Serge's attitude toward problems of theory were serious, he would have been embarrassed to come to the fore as an "innovator" and to pull us back to Bernstein, Struve, and all the revisionists of the last century who tried to graft Kantianism onto Marxism, or in other words, to subordinate the class struggle of the proletariat to principles allegedly rising above it. As did Kant himself, they depicted the "categorical imperative" (the idea of duty) as an absolute norm of morality valid for everybody. In reality, it is a question of "duty" to bourgeois society. In their own fashion, Bernstein, Struve, Vorlander, had a serious attitude toward theory. They openly demanded a *return* to Kant. Victor Serge and his compeers do not feel the slightest responsibility towards scientific thought. They confine themselves to allusions, insinuations, at best, to literary generalizations. . . . However, if their ideas are plumbed to the bottom, it appears that they have joined an old cause, long since discredited: to subdue Marxism by means of Kantianism; to paralyze the socialist revolution by means of "absolute" norms which represent in reality the philosophical generalizations of the interests of the bourgeoisie — true enough, not the present-day but the defunct bourgeoisie of the era of free trade and democracy. The imperialist bourgeoisie observes these norms even less than did its liberal grandmother. But it views favorably the attempts of the petty-bourgeois preachers to introduce confusion, turbulence, and vacillation into the ranks of the revolutionary proletariat. The chief aim not only of Hitler but also of the liberals and the democrats is to discredit Bolshevism at a time when its historical legitimacy threatens to become absolutely clear to the masses. Bolshevism, Marxism — there is the enemy!

When "Brother" Victor Basch, high priest of democratic morality, with the aid of his "Brother" Rosenmark, committed a forgery in defense of the Moscow trials, he was publicly exposed. Convicted of falsehood, he beat his breast and cried: "Am I then partial? I have always denounced the terror of Lenin and Trotsky." Basch graphically exposed the inner mainspring of the moralists of democracy: Some of them may keep quiet about the Moscow trials, some may attack the trials, still others may defend the trials; but their common concern is to use the trials in condemning the "morality" of Lenin and

Trotsky, that is, the methods of the proletarian revolution. In this sphere they are all brothers.

In the above-cited scandalous prospectus it is stated that I develop views on morality "basing" myself "on Lenin." This indefinite phrase, reproduced by other publications, can be taken to mean that I develop Lenin's theoretical principles. But to my knowledge Lenin did not write on morality. Victor Serge wished in reality to say something altogether different, namely, that my immoral ideas are a generalization of the practice of Lenin, the "amoralist." He seeks to discredit Lenin's personality by my judgments, and my judgments by the personality of Lenin. He is simply flattering the general reactionary tendency, which is aimed against Bolshevism and Marxism as a whole.

Souvarine, the sycophant

Ex-pacifist, ex-communist, ex-Trotskyist, ex-democrato-communist, ex-Marxist . . . almost ex-Souvarine attacks the proletarian revolution and revolutionists all the more brazenly the less he himself knows what he wants. This man loves and knows how to collect quotations, documents, commas, and quotation marks and how to compile dossiers and, moreover, he knows how to handle the pen. Originally he had hoped that this baggage would last him a lifetime. But he was soon compelled to convince himself that in addition the ability to think was necessary. . . . His book on Stalin, despite an abundance of interesting quotations and facts, is a self-testimonial to his own poverty. Souvarine understands neither what the revolution is nor what the counterrevolution is. He applies to the historical process the criteria of a petty rationalizer, forever aggrieved at sinful humanity. The disproportion between his critical spirit and his creative impotence consumes him as if it were an acid. Hence his constant exasperation, and his lack of elementary honesty in appraising ideas, people, and events, while covering it all with dry moralizing. Like all misanthropes and cynics, Souvarine is organically drawn toward reaction.

Has Souvarine broken openly with Marxism? We never heard about it. He prefers equivocation; that is his native element. In his review of my pamphlet he writes: "Trotsky once again mounts his hobby-horse of the class struggle." To the Marxist of yesterday the class struggle is — "Trotsky's hobby-horse." It is not surprising that Souvarine himself has preferred to sit astride the dead dog of eternal morality. To the Marxist conception he opposes "a sense of justice . . . without regard for class distinctions." It is at any rate consoling to learn that our society is founded on a "sense of justice." In the coming war Souvarine will doubtless expound his discovery to the soldiers in the trenches; and in the meantime he can do so to the invalids of the last war, the unemployed, the abandoned children, and the prostitutes. We confess in advance that should he get mauled while thus engaged, our own "sense of justice" will not side with him. . . .

The critical remarks of this shameless apologist for bourgeois justice "without regard for class distinctions," are based entirely on . . . the prospectus inspired by Victor Serge. The latter, in his turn, in all his attempts at "theory" does not go beyond hybrid borrowings from Souvarine, who, nevertheless, possesses this advantage: that he utters what Serge does not yet dare to say.

With feigned indignation — there is nothing genuine about him — Souvarine writes that inasmuch as Trotsky condemns the morality of democrats, reformists, Stalinists, and anarchists, it follows that the sole representative of morality is "Trotsky's party," and since this party "does not exist," therefore in the last analysis the incarnation of morality is Trotsky himself. How can one help tittering over this? Souvarine apparently imagines that he is capable of distinguishing between that which exists and that which does not. It is a very simple matter so long as it is a question of scrambled eggs or a pair of suspenders. But on the scale of the historical process such a distinction is obviously over Souvarine's head. "That which exists" is being born or dying, developing or disintegrating. That which exists can be understood only by those who understand its inner tendencies.

The number of people who held a revolutionary position at the outbreak of the last war could be counted on one's fingers. The entire field of official politics was almost completely pervaded with various shades of chauvinism. Liebknecht, Luxemburg, Lenin, seemed impotent, isolated individuals. But can there be any doubt that their morality was above the bestial morality of the "sacred union"? Liebknecht's revolutionary politics was not at all "individualistic," as then seemed to the average patriotic philistine. On the contrary, Liebknecht, and Liebknecht alone, reflected and foreshadowed the profound subterranean trends in the masses. The subsequent course of events wholly confirmed this. Not to fear today a complete break with official public opinion so as on the *morrow* to gain the right of expressing the ideas and feelings of the insurgent masses, this is a special mode of existence which differs from the empiric existence of petty-bourgeois conventionalists. All the parties of capitalist society, all its moralists and all its sycophants will perish beneath the debris of the impending catastrophe. The only party that will survive is the party of the world socialist revolution, even though it may seem nonexistent today to the sightless rationalizers, just as during the last war the party of Lenin and Liebknecht seemed to them nonexistent.

Revolutionists and the carriers of infection

Engels once wrote that Marx and himself remained all their lives in the minority and "felt fine" about it. Periods when the movement of the oppressed class rises to the level of the general tasks of the revolution represent the rarest exceptions in history. Far more frequent than victories are the defeats of the oppressed. Following each defeat comes a long period of reaction, which throws the revolutionists back into a state of cruel isolation. Pseudorevolutionists, "knights for an hour," as a Russian poet put it, either openly betray the cause of the oppressed in such periods or scurry about in search of a formula of salvation that would enable them to avoid breaking with any of the camps. It is inconceivable in our time to find a conciliatory formula in the sphere of political economy or sociology; class contradictions have forever overthrown the "harmony" formula of the liberals and democratic reformers. There remains the domain of religion and transcendental morality. The Russian Social Revolutionaries attempted to save democracy by an alliance with the church. Marceau Pivert replaces the church with Freemasonry. Apparently, Victor Serge has not yet joined a lodge, but he has no difficulty in finding a common language with Pivert against Marxism.

Two classes decide the fate of modern society: the imperialist bourgeoisie and the proletariat. The last resource of the bourgeoisie is fascism, which replaces social and historical criteria with biological and zoological standards so as thus to free itself from any and all restrictions in the struggle for capitalist property. Civilization can be saved only by the socialist revolution. To accomplish the overturn, the proletariat needs all its strength, all its resolution, all its audacity, passion, and ruthlessness. Above all it must be completely free from the fictions of religion, "democracy," and transcendental morality — the spiritual chains forged by the enemy to tame and enslave it. Only that which prepares the complete and final overthrow of imperialist bestiality is moral, and nothing else. The welfare of the revolution — that is the supreme law!

A clear understanding of the interrelation between the two basic classes — the bourgeoisie and the proletariat in the epoch of their mortal combat — discloses to us the objective meaning of the role of petty-bourgeois moralists. Their chief trait is impotence: *social* impotence by virtue of the economic degradation of the petty bourgeoisie;

ideological impotence by virtue of the fear of the petty bourgeoisie in the face of the monstrous unleashing of the class struggle. Hence the urge of the petty bourgeois, both educated and ignorant, to curb the class struggle. If he cannot succeed by means of eternal morality — and this cannot succeed — the petty bourgeois throws himself into the arms of fascism, which curbs the class struggle by means of myths and the executioner's axe. The moralism of V. Serge and his compeers is a bridge from revolution to reaction. Souvarine is already on the other side of the bridge. The slightest concession to these tendencies signifies the beginning of capitulation to reaction. Let these carriers of infection instil the rules of morality in Hitler, Mussolini, Chamberlain, and Daladier. As for us, the program of the proletarian revolution suffices.

Coyoacan, June 9, 1939

Means and Ends
by John Dewey

The relation of means and ends has long been an outstanding issue in morals. It has also been a burning issue in political theory and practice. Of late the discussion has centered about the later developments of Marxism in the USSR. The course of the Stalinists has been defended by many of his adherents in other countries on the ground that the purges and prosecutions, perhaps even with a certain amount of falsification, was necessary to maintain the alleged socialistic regime of that country. Others have used the measures of the Stalinist bureaucracy to condemn the Marxist policy on the ground that the latter leads to such excesses as have occurred in the USSR precisely because Marxism holds that the end justifies the means. Some of these critics have held that since Trotsky is also a Marxian he is committed to the same policy and consequently if he had been in power would also have felt bound to use any means whatever that seemed necessary to achieve the end involved in dictatorship by the proletariat.

The discussion has had at least one useful theoretical result. It has brought out into the open for the first time, as far as I am aware, an explicit discussion by a consistent Marxian on the relation of means and ends in social action.* At the courteous invitation of one of the editors of this review, I propose to discuss this issue in the light of Mr. Trotsky's discussion of the interdependence of means and ends. Much of the earlier part of his essay

---

* *Their Morals and Ours,* by Leon Trotsky, The New International, June 1938, pp. 163-73.

67

does not, accordingly, enter into my discussion, though I may say that on the ground of *tu quoque* argument (suggested by the title) Trotsky has had no great difficulty in showing that some of his critics have acted in much the same way they attribute to him. Since Mr. Trotsky also indicates that the only alternative position to the idea that the end justifies the means is some form of absolutistic ethics based on the alleged deliverances of conscience, or a moral sense, or some brand of eternal truths, I wish to say that I write from a standpoint that rejects all such doctrines as definitely as does Mr. Trotsky himself, and that I hold that the end in the sense of consequences provides the only basis for moral ideas and action, and therefore provides the only justification that can be found for means employed.

The point I propose to consider is that brought up toward the end of Mr. Trotsky's discussion in the section headed "Dialectic Interdependence of Means and Ends." The following statement is basic: "A means can be justified only by its end. But the end in turn needs to be justified. From the Marxian point of view, which expresses the historic interests of the proletariat, the end is justified if it leads to increasing the power of man over nature and to the abolition of the power of man over man" (p. 172). This increase of the power of man over nature, accompanying the abolition of the power of man over man, seems accordingly to be *the* end — that is, an end which does not need itself to be justified but which is the justification of the ends that are in turn means to it. It may also be added that others than Marxians might accept this formulation of *the* end and hold it expresses the moral interest of society — if not the historic interest — and not merely and exclusively that of the proletariat.

But for my present purpose, it is important to note that the word *"end"* is here used to cover two things — the final justifying end and ends that are themselves means to this final end. For while it is not said in so many words that some ends are but means, that proposition is certainly implied in the statement that some ends "*lead to* increasing the power of man over nature, *etc.*" Mr. Trotsky goes on to explain that the principle that the end justifies the means does not mean that every means is permissible. "That is permissible, we answer, which really leads to the liberation of mankind."

Were the latter statement consistently adhered to and followed through it would be consistent with the sound principle of interdependence of means and end. Being in accord with it, it would lead to scrupulous examination of the means that are used, to ascertain what their actual objective consequences will be as far as it is humanly possible to tell — to show that they do "really" lead to the liberation of mankind. It is at this point that the double significance of *end* becomes important. As far as it means consequences actually reached, it is clearly dependent upon means used, while measures in their capacity of means are dependent upon the end in the sense that they have to be viewed and judged on the ground of their actual objective results. On this basis, an *end-in-view* represents or is an *idea* of the final consequences, in case the idea is formed *on the ground of the means that are judged to be most likely to produce the end*. The end-in-view is thus itself a means for directing action — just as a man's *idea* of health to be attained or a house to be built is not identical with *end* in the sense of actual outcome but is a means for directing action to achieve that end.

Now what has given the maxim (and the practice it formulates) that the end justifies the means a bad name is that the end-in-view, the end professed and entertained (perhaps quite sincerely) justifies the use of certain means, and so justifies the latter that it is not necessary to examine what the actual consequences of the use of chosen means will be. An individual may hold, and quite sincerely as far as his personal opinion is concerned, that certain means will "really" lead to a professed and desired end. But the real question is not one of personal belief but of the objective grounds upon which it is held: namely, the consequences that will actually be produced by them. So when Mr. Trotsky says that "dialectical materialism knows no dualism between means and end," the natural interpretation is that he will recommend the use of means that can be shown by their own nature to lead to the liberation of mankind as an objective consequence.

One would expect, then, that with the idea of the liberation of mankind as the end-in-view, there would be an examination of *all* means that are likely to attain this end without any fixed preconception as to what they *must* be, and that every suggested means would be weighed and judged on the express ground of the consequences it is likely to produce.

But this is *not* the course adopted in Mr. Trotsky's further discussion. He says: "The liberating morality of the proletariat is of a revolutionary character. . . . It *deduces* a rule of conduct from the laws of the development of society, thus primarily from the class struggle, the law of all laws" (italics are mine). As if to leave no doubt of his meaning he says: "The end flows from the historical movement"—that of the class struggle. The principle of interdependence of means and end has thus disappeared or at least been submerged. For the choice of means is not decided upon on the ground of an independent examination of measures and policies with respect to their actual objective consequences. On the contrary, means are *"deduced"* from an independent source, an alleged law of history which is *the* law of all laws of social development. Nor does the logic of the case change if the word "alleged" is stricken out. For even so, it follows that means to be used are not derived from consideration of the end, the liberation of mankind, but from another outside source. The professed end — the end-in-view — the liberation of mankind, is thus subordinated to the class struggle as the means by which it is to be attained. Instead of *inter*-dependence of means and end, the end is dependent upon the means but the

means are not derived from the end. Since the class struggle is regarded as the *only* means that will reach the
end, and since the view that it is the only means is reached
deductively and not by an inductive examination of the
means-consequences in their interdependence, the means,
the class struggle, does not need to be critically examined
with respect to its actual objective consequences. It is
automatically absolved from all need for critical examination. If we are not back in the position that the *end-
in-view* (as distinct from objective consequences) justifies
the use of any means in line with the class struggle and
that it justifies the neglect of all other means, I fail to
understand the logic of Mr. Trotsky's position.

The position that I have indicated as that of genuine
interdependence of means and ends does not automatically
rule out class struggle as one means for attaining the
end. But it does rule out the deductive method of arriving
at it as a means, to say nothing of its being the *only*
means. The selection of class struggle as a means has
to be justified, on the ground of the interdependence of
means and end, by an examination of actual consequences
of its use, not deductively. Historical considerations are
certainly relevant to this examination. But the assumption
of a *fixed law* of social development is not relevant. It
is as if a biologist or a physician were to assert that
a certain law of biology which he accepts is so related
to the end of health that the means of arriving at health —
the only means — can be deduced from it, so that no
further examination of biological phenomena is needed.
The whole case is prejudged.

It is one thing to say that class struggle is a means
of attaining the end of the liberation of mankind. It is
a radically different thing to say that there is an absolute
law of class struggle which determines the means to be
used. For if it determines the means, it also determines
the end — the actual consequence, and upon the principle
of genuine interdependence of means and end it is arbi-
trary and subjective to say that that consequence will

be the liberation of mankind. The liberation of mankind is the end to be striven for. In any legitimate sense of "moral," it is a moral end. No scientific law can determine a moral end save by deserting the principle of interdependence of means and end. A Marxian may sincerely believe that class struggle is *the* law of social development. But quite aside from the fact that the belief closes the doors to further examination of history — just as an assertion that the Newtonian laws are the final laws of physics would preclude further search for physical laws — it would not follow, even if it were *the* scientific law of history, that it is the means to the moral goal of the liberation of mankind. That it is such a means has to be shown not by "deduction" from a law but by examination of means and consequences; an examination in which, given the liberation of mankind as end, there is free and unprejudiced search for the means by which it can be attained.

One more consideration may be added about class struggle as a means. There are presumably several, perhaps many, different ways by means of which the class struggle may be carried on. How can a choice be made among these different ways except by examining their consequences in relation to the goal of liberation of mankind? The belief that a law of history determines the particular way in which the struggle is to be carried on certainly seems to tend toward a fanatical and even mystical devotion to use of certain ways of conducting the class struggle to the exclusion of all other ways of conducting it. I have no wish to go outside the theoretical question of the interdependence of means and ends, but it is conceivable that the course actually taken by the revolution in the USSR becomes more explicable when it is noted that means were deduced from a supposed scientific law instead of being searched for and adopted on the ground of their relation to the moral end of the liberation of mankind.

The only conclusion I am able to reach is that in

avoiding one kind of absolutism Mr. Trotsky has plunged into another kind of absolutism. There appears to be a curious transfer among orthodox Marxists of allegiance from the ideals of socialism and scientific *methods* of attaining them (scientific in the sense of being based on the objective relations of means and consequences) to the class struggle as the law of historical change. Deduction of ends set up, of means and attitudes, from this law as the primary thing makes all moral questions, that is, all questions of the end to be finally attained, meaningless. To be scientific about ends does not mean to read them out of laws, whether the laws are natural or social. Orthodox Marxism shares with orthodox religionism and with traditional idealism the belief that human ends are interwoven into the very texture and structure of existence — a conception inherited presumably from its Hegelian origin.

New York City, July 3, 1938

Liberal Morality

The controversy between
John Dewey and Leon Trotsky
by George Novack

American liberals are convinced that their positions are far stronger than those of the Marxists on both the lofty plane of ethical theory and in practical morality. They have persuaded many others that this is so. Stalin's terror regime, climaxed by the frame-up executions of the Old Bolsheviks in the Moscow trials, gave the democrats a field day to parade their moral superiority not only over the Stalinists but also over the revolutionary socialists who were their victims. In the late 1930s a debate boiled up in various intellectual circles throughout the globe on the problem of the relations between ethics and politics, until the blood-soaked exhibition of morality presented by capitalist imperialism in the Second World War cut it short.

The hearings held in April 1937 by the International Commission of Inquiry into the Moscow Trials at Coyoacan, Mexico, had touched upon these questions in passing. Soon afterward Trotsky wrote an essay, *Their Morals and Ours,* which appeared in *The New International* of June 1938. The philosopher-educator John Dewey, head of the commission which had cleared Trotsky of the charges against him, wrote a criticism of Trotsky's ideas entitled *Means and Ends,* which was printed in the same magazine in August of that year. The press of other work prevented Trotsky from undertaking the rejoinder he wanted to make to Dewey's arguments.

This inconclusive debate between the foremost spokesmen for pragmatism and Marxism was a rare direct confrontation of the fundamental views of the two philosophies on the moral aspects of social and political action. This question has not lost its pertinence or ceased to command the attention of liberals and rebels in the twenty-seven years since. Indeed, it is more timely today than then.

Problems of ethics

Before coming to grips with the issues of method raised in that ideological encounter, it may be helpful to survey the fundamental problems involved in formulating a critical and rational ethics.

Theoreticians of morality confront two principal difficulties in arriving at a rational foundation or scientific explanation for standards of conduct. One is the extreme variability in the notions of right and wrong through the ages. It would be hard to find a human action which has not been subject to opposing moral judgments. Devouring human beings is today universally condemned — and yet it was universally practiced in primeval times. Some food-gathering and hunting tribes put old people to death; nowadays we strive to prolong their lives.

Freedom in sexual relations, which is today illegal, was at one time prevalent and approved. Although it is considered wrong to lie, such paragons of ethics as doctors dispute, in general and concrete cases, whether it is right to tell the truth about his condition to a patient stricken with a fatal disease. The grossly unequal ownership and distribution of wealth which is taken for granted under capitalism would have been condemned by the primitive Indians. These illustrations could be multiplied.

Even worse for seekers of the absolute in morality is the fact that the very same features of an action which are the highest good for one set of people are at the very same time supreme evils for another. Strikebreakers are heroes to the bosses but villains to the workers. Stool pigeons are praised by the witch-hunters and execrated by their political and union victims. The atom-bombing of Hiroshima and Nagasaki, which horrified Asia, was justified by the Allied powers. As Cuba has lately driven home to us, the expropriation of private property evokes contrary moral judgments from the defenders of capitalism and the proponents of socialism.

In view of such conflicting moral situations which involve the coexistence of contradictory appraisals of the same acts and actors, what solid grounds can there be for discriminating good from bad, right from wrong? Are stable moral standards at all possible?

Every school of ethics has presented its own answer to these questions. The traditional religions offer a divine justification for their mildewed moralities. The injunctions of their codes are claimed to be God's word as revealed by Moses, Christ, Mohammed and interpreted by rabbis, priests, and other authorized church officials. God's commandments are eternal and cannot be violated with impunity because they are the passports to heaven and immortality.

Morality has gradually been liberated from such religious sanctions. With the advance of civilization, more enlightened culture, and scientific knowledge, philosophers have had to devise rational and secular bases for ethics. Once morality had been dislodged from anchorage in Heaven, it was necessary to find the reasons for its existence and evolution in the changing needs of human beings as these have progressed on earth. Historical materialism finally provided the most valid scientific explanation for the origins and substance of moral codes, their social functions and their limitations.

The Marxist conception of morality

"Men, consciously or unconsciously, derive their moral ideas in the last resort from the practical relations on which their class position is based — from the economic relations in which they carry on production and exchange," stated Engels in his exposition of the Marxist theory of morality in *Anti-Duehring*. The morality of tribal life necessarily differs in its fundamental values from those of civilized societies because of the basic differences in their productive relations and forms of property. The commandment forbidding stealing or coveting a neighbor's wife appears ridiculous to primitive people who are not bound by the customs of private ownership either in the instruments of production or the agents of reproduction.

Engels pointed out that three principal moralities are in vogue today. There is Christian-feudal morality, best exemplified by Catholicism; modern bourgeois morality; and proletarian morality. Their attitudes toward marriage and divorce can serve to illustrate the differences in these moral viewpoints. To the Catholic, marriages are "made in heaven" and should endure forever; to the ordinary bourgeois, wedlock is the result of a civil contract validated, regulated or terminated by government officials; to the socialist, it is a personal matter to be entered into or ended by the free will of the persons concerned.

These general moral outlooks represent three successive stages in the development of economic relations and express the needs and views of different class formations and social systems. They coexist and contend with one another in people's minds and lives today.

Engels concluded that all moralities and their theoretical justifications have been products of the economic stage society reached at that particular epoch. Since civilized society has hitherto moved in class antagonisms and continues to do so, all morality has been and must necessarily be class morality. "It has either justified the domination and interests of the ruling class, or, as soon as the oppressed class becomes powerful enough, it has represented the revolt against this domination and the future interests of the oppressed." Thus his materialist explanation for the changes and diversity in moral judgments also provides the justification for new and higher ones.

The ethical approach of pragmatism

The pragmatists consider themselves specialists on matters of morality. Moral theory is, on the one hand, their substitute for conventional religion; on the other hand, it provides their major means of defense and offense against a thoroughly materialist approach to social problems.

The pragmatists do not lean upon any "eternal verities" as a sanction for moral standards. They understand that these have been irretrievably battered down by the theory of evolution and the acquisitions of modern knowledge. On what grounds, then, can the practice of any virtues be recommended and justified? They are not good in and of themselves, or divinely inspired like the Ten Commandments, or enforced by taboos. According to John Dewey, the worth of any action, any course of conduct or policy is to be judged solely and simply by its real consequences. What counts is not the intentions, motives, or aims of individuals but the concrete results which flow from people's actions. Dewey conceives of morality as "overt activity having consequences instead of as mere inner personal attribute" (*The Quest for Certainty*, p. 6). This *objective* criterion separated Dewey from all the semi-religious and sentimental souls for whom moral worth depends upon "goodness of heart."

Whatever actions tend to increase wealth and equalize its distribution, extend democracy and freedom, institute peaceful relations, open more opportunities for more people, enhance their sensitivities, add to their understanding, etc., are good. If they have the contrary consequences, they must be condemned as immoral.

Thus exploitation is wrong because it robs, divides, and oppresses people — and the exploiters should be made to recognize that and either correct themselves or be corrected by the community. Force is wrong, or rather, far more often pernicious than helpful in its results. It must therefore not be resorted to — or at least employed only sparingly in case of overwhelming necessity. Class conflict is wrong — and ought to be replaced by class harmony and collaboration.

Such dicta show great good will and testify to the benevolence of the pragmatic moralist. But they do not promote a scientific understanding of the real situation which has created these social conflicts, nor do they indicate a practical solution for them. It is cheap to rail against the rich and say the privileged must consider the needs of the poor and take measures to relieve them. Religion has preached such sermons — and practiced such charity — for many centuries without eradicating the conditions which generate inequality.

There is a vast difference between such abstract moralizing and a genuinely scientific investigation of morality and its development. A scientific approach to morality should be able to inform us, not only that exploitation is evil, but why the rich must act that way in the first place, and thereby indicate how the evils of exploitation can be removed. This is not an individual but a collective social problem.

The highest aim of any humanist ethics is the self-realization of each individual, the development and perfecting of the human personality. Dewey correctly recognized that individual conduct is perforce subordinate to social action and that morality is indissolubly bound up with social conditions, conduct, and consequences. He was willing to pose the issue and do battle with Marxism in behalf of his own viewpoint on that advanced arena.

Means and ends in morality

The first question he tackled was the thorny one of the relation between means and ends in morality. Many liberal moralizers believe that such a maxim is the root of all evil. It may therefore come as a shock and surprise to them that Dewey agreed with Trotsky that the end justifies the means. The ends and means are interdependent.

But neither one, said Dewey, can be justified by "alleged deliverances of conscience, or a moral sense, or some brand of eternal truths." They can be justified, he declared, only by their actual results. "I hold that the end in the sense of consequences provides the only basis for moral ideas and action and therefore provides the only justification that can be found for means employed." Nothing else can make means good or bad but the outcome of their use.

Trotsky had stated that the ultimate ends of socialist action are the increase of the power of man over nature and the abolition, as a consequence, of the power of man over man (social oppression). Dewey, too, regarded these as the worthiest of objectives. Trotsky further stated that all those means that contributed to the realization of these aims are morally justified. So far, there was no disagreement between the Marxist and the pragmatist.

Their positions parted when the questions of the agencies and roads through which these goals were to be achieved were brought under consideration. Trotsky asserted that the only force in modern society capable of carrying through this job was the organized working class. The only way labor can eliminate oppression and complete the conquest of nature was by developing to the very end its struggles against the capitalist beneficiaries and upholders of economic privilege.

Here Dewey took sharp issue with him. Both of these propositions were wrong, he replied. Trotsky was not warranted in entrusting the fundamental tasks of social reconstruction in our epoch to the workers. This is a matter of common concern which surpasses any special class interests. All people of good will from the topmost level of society to the lowest should be mobilized in joint effort to secure collective control over nature and our economy.

Trotsky also erred, claimed Dewey, in his exclusive reliance upon the prosecution of the class struggle as the means of arriving at the desired goals. Other ways and means than hurling capitalists and workers against one another are not only as good but will bring better results.

Thus their differences over moral theory revolved around disagreements over the agents and the means of social advancement. In essence, it was a dispute over *method:* both method of thought and method of conduct.

Dewey himself deliberately elevated their dispute to the level of logical method and scientific procedure. Trotsky's method of reasoning is incorrect, Dewey said, because he *deduced* the means (the class struggle) from his reading (or misreading) of the course of social development. By illegitimately erecting the class struggle into the supreme and absolute law of history, Trotsky actually subordinated the ends to a particular means instead of permitting the ends to determine the means. How should Trotsky have derived the means? "By an examination of actual consequences of its use," wrote Dewey. This is the only genuinely scientific approach which takes into account the real interdependence of the two factors.

To *deduction,* the extraction of particular conclusions from general rules, Dewey counterposed the procedure of *induction,* the arriving at generalizations on the basis of repeated duplicated instances.

This antithesis is an unfounded one. Did Trotsky actually derive his means arbitrarily, as Dewey implied, through deductive processes alone? To be sure, Trotsky did explicitly evaluate means by reference to the laws and needs of the class struggle. These laws, however, were not freely created and imposed upon society by the Marxists. They had been drawn from a prior comprehensive study of social processes over many generations by strictly scientific methods. The laws of class struggle are first of all *empirical* generalizations developed from analysis of the *facts* presented by the history of civilization, including American history.

The logical status of the class struggle

The impressive array of factual materials regarding class conflict and its crucial role in history from which these laws are derived were observed and recorded long before Marx arrived on the scene. For instance, many ancient Greek writers and historians (Thucydides, Aris-

totle, Plato) noted and described them. What the historical materialists did was to give the first adequate and
correct explanation of them. They explained how classes originated through the growth of the productive forces,
the division of social labor, and the existence of a size-
able surplus of products, and why class conflicts have
revolved around the mode of appropriation of this ex-
panding surplus of wealth.

Is this no more than a hypothesis about social development? That is what Dewey, the instrumentalist, wished
to say. But the class struggle has had a different role
than the dubious one liberals assign to it. It is much more
than a mere possibility or a chance and episodic occurrence in civilized life. It is a necessity, a certainity. It
proceeds according to a verified set of laws which formulate fundamental factors arising from the innermost
constitution of class society. These apply to all types
of class societies regardless of their levels of development and specific peculiarities. *

Once the laws governing the class struggle had been
discovered, formulated and verified, they could be applied
like all other scientific laws. They enabled investigators
to probe more deeply into the structure and inner movements of society, its groupings and leading personali-
ties and thus anticipate and, under certain circumstances,
direct its developments to a certain extent.

The nature of concepts and laws

Instrumentalists like Dewey, however, have an iron preconception against even the most solidly based prejudg-

---

* This reality was recognized not long ago by certain worker-
priests in France who had been sent by the Church among the
workers to combat the godless materialist heresies of Marxism.
"We have learned," they wrote in a letter to Cardinal Feltin,
October 5, 1953, "that the class struggle is not a mere principle that one can accept or refuse, but that it is a brutal fact
which is imposed upon the working class." Because of their
refusal to recant, they were unfrocked. — G. N.

ments. This aversion is a prime principle of their theory of knowledge which has a built-in contradiction. The instrumentalists rightly insist upon the universal changeability of all things. Yet for them ideas maintain a curiously static essence through thick or thin. Ideas do not lose their inherently *hypothetical* character and can never really change into certainties, whatever the course and results of social and scientific development.

This assumption is neither empirical nor rational. In reality, many ideas which begin as hypotheses turn into something quite different as the result of scientific inquiry and verified practice. They become tested truths, scientific laws. The theory of the existence of atoms and the inner atomic structure of matter was only a brilliant guess, an intuition, when it was first propounded in ancient Greece. Nowadays it has become a validated truth from which it is possible to derive the most explosive consequences. Yet for Dewey, like the positivist Ernst Mach, the atom was not a reality but only an "operational idea." (See *Logic*, p. 153, and *The Quest for Certainty*, pp. 119 and 131.)

Dewey objected that the laws of the class struggle are not soundly based because they "prejudge the characteristic traits and the kinds of actual phenomena that the proposed plans of action are to deal with." But they do so no more and no less than the laws of atomic activity or any other physical laws.

For pure pragmatists all conceptual generalizations remain perpetually on trial. No decisive verdict on their truth or falsity can ever be rendered by any judge, no matter how qualified, no matter how great the amount of evidence. Why? Because indeterminate elements can never be totally eliminated from reality and therefore what is provisional and inconclusive can never be excluded from scientific thought.

For them every conception has to be freshly evaluated, and every conclusion revalidated from top to bottom, in every new situation. Its thousandth repetition has no qualitatively different or more coercive character than the original occurrence. The instrumentalists talk as though it were possible, and necessary, for people to start afresh on every occasion, confronting the world around them empty-handed and empty-headed.

This is essentially a denial of the value of all acquired knowledge, all scientific methods, and even of the results of induction. No one but an infant reacts to the world and tackles the problems it presents without using the accumulated resources of social development, including the growing fund of prejudgments derived from historical experience and from the direct examination of reality.

These are not a mass of mere speculations; they consist by and large of authenticated information and tested generalizations. But in the eyes of the instrumentalists, for whom, if they are consistent, "ideas do not disclose reality," the content of ideas remains essentially indeterminate and forever hypothetical.

The progress of science leads to the acquisition of knowledge of the real forces which determine the production of phenomena and their subsequent formulation into laws. Dewey immensely exaggerated the aspect of indeterminateness in reality and the uncertainty of genuine knowledge. He underestimated and even excluded on principle knowing in advance and acting on ascertained truths about real situations.

"Every measure of policy is logically, and should be actually, of the nature of an experiment," he insisted in his *Logic* (p. 508). This sweeping assertion is neither logically correct nor factually complete. It is a dangerous and misleading half-truth.

It depends upon the concrete circumstances of a situation and the nature of the proposal made whether or not a given policy is essentially, or only incidentally, "in the nature of an experiment." In most cases there is, to be sure, an inescapable measure of indeterminacy which endows the reaction to it with a questionable character. But this measure of uncertainty, of contingency, is quantitatively and qualitatively variable. The value of scientific theory and the aim of rational practice is to reduce this to the minimum.

Let us take two examples from industrial practice. A lathe operator in a factory can know in advance whether a bit is too soft to cut steel of a certain hardness. He would not use a softer steel, and certainly not a wooden peg, for that purpose. In this case the end — the machining of metal to a certain shape and size — and the material reality — the hardness of the metal — reciprocally determine beforehand, both positively and negatively, the type of means for attaining the desired product.

Why cannot the same rules apply to industrial relations as to shop practice? Can't the same worker know in advance how his employer will react when he and his associates ask for a raise in wages? The employer is a social reality of a certain type. His material interests give him a specific degree of hardness, a determined resistance to having his costs of production increased and his profits cut. In order to attain their ends, his workers need social instruments of a certain kind, strong enough to overcome that resistance. That is why they have organized unions and engage in strikes instead of relying upon individual petition.

Here we come to the nub of the problem. Every wage negotiation is not and need not be a totally fresh experiment with unknown factors, whatever may be the uncertainties in any given situation. Workers and employers have been dealing with one another for many scores of years all over the world. An experienced union leadership and an informed membership can enter collective bargaining forearmed with knowledge of the bosses' nature gained from social science and everyday experience which helps to handle opposition to the just demands of the workers.

If every negotiation or every act of production were to be approached in theory or in practice as wholly or largely experimental, as Dewey demands, then no particular means can be regarded beforehand as necessarily better or more suited to the requirements of the struggle than any other. This excludes reliance upon verified procedures and leaves the field wide open to any capricious innovation.

Such unrestricted and uncontrolled experimentalism is utterly alien to the actual procedures of scientists and to the normal methods of modern industry. The aim of automated factory production is to leave nothing to chance, but to regulate all the factors in the process. Accidents, exceptions occur in the best-regulated systems. But even these are anticipated by instruments installed in advance to detect these variations when they depart from permissible limits and then to compensate for and correct them in time. Self-regulating systems are especially imperative for such industrial complexes as atomic nuclear plants which embody the highest union of scientific theory and production.

Dewey said he wanted the most up-to-date methods of science and industry extended into everyday affairs. If this is done, then the field of operation for random experiment in the most vital areas of social life ought to be reduced and itself made subject to control. Experiment is necessary in all spheres of activity. Both science and industry take care of this need by providing special places for the conduct of experiments. In industry experimental work in pilot plants, laboratories, and in the field is carefully segregated from mass production which is carried out with already verified techniques and machinery.

In modern times there have been countless experiences, and even experiments, made by contending social forces in the domain of class relations. The positive and negative results of these various methods of action have been summarized by scientific socialism in the laws of the class struggle and codified in the programs of workers' parties. These have great practical value as guides to progressive social forces in their struggles.

The pragmatic viewpoint, on the other hand, is based

upon the *formal* equality of all ideas rather than on their real material standing. Any idea is regarded as in itself just as true, useful, and effective as any other. In the same way the commodity market is presumed to rest upon the formal equality of exchanges; bourgeois law, upon the formal equality of all citizens before the bar of justice; and its democracy, upon the equally decisive vote of all citizens. All these assumptions contradict the real state of affairs in capitalist society with its economic inequalities and class differentials.

One idea is not in reality as good as another. Some are truer and better than others because they do not all reflect reality equally well or widely and therefore do not have the same consequences when used to direct activity.

The mutual determinism of ends and means

For Dewey the ends and the means are interdependent. But he believed that these two terms merely *condition* one another; neither one can determine the other or be predetermined by sufficient material conditions. The one is as conditional and hypothetical as the other.

For example, exploitation is bad and must be eliminated. But for Dewey it may be uprooted in any number of ways: by class struggle, by class agreement, or by a combination of both. None of these means is decisive for accomplishing the desired aim: the abolition of capitalist exploitation. Such is his abstract theoretical position.

This appears to be thoroughly impartial. But when it comes to practice—which, after all, is the decisive test for the pragmatist—the liberal is not so unbiased. By disposition he prefers, and in nine instances out of ten chooses, the methods of least resistance. The line of most resistance is always his last resort. This bias is not accidental. It flows from the necessity of his nature as a social being, his interests and outlook as a middle class intellectual, the ambiguity of being in the middle of opposing social camps.

Sometimes the left liberal does take the road of struggle—but only grudgingly and under the compulsion of overriding circumstances. He feels that this method is somehow out of tune with reality and the best interests of all concerned, including his own. In reality, class-struggle methods are simply inconsistent with his in-between position where he is pulled in opposite directions by the antagonisms between capital and labor, white and black.

Dewey's second major criticism of Trotsky is that Marxists are absolutistic in appealing to fixed laws for their choice of means of social action. Trotsky, he claimed, was not being empirical or scientific but idealistic and religious-minded because he imposed his desired aims upon social development and acted as though "human ends are interwoven into the very texture and structure of existence."

How much justification is there to this criticism? As a materialist, Trotsky never believed that *human* ends are interwoven into *nature's* existence. He did assert, however, that *class* ends are objectively woven "into the very texture and structure" of *social* existence under certain historical circumstances.

Dewey denied this. For him society does not have so determinate a texture and structure that any general laws on the objectives of classes can be obtained from an analysis of social development and subsequently used to calculate their conduct as a basis for action.

If there are no definite laws governing the activities of classes, then there can be no necessary means, like the class struggle, to attain social objectives. If there are neither ascertainable laws nor prescribed means, then what takes their place? Tentative guesses, hopeful and wishful plans, experimental efforts. Before the act, many different kinds of means, and in principle almost any means, may achieve the ends-in-view. If you don't know where you are going or what you are really up against, any road will presumably take you there.

On what grounds, then, should one means be selected

over others? Of course Dewey acknowledges that previous knowledge and experience is to be used in the process of selection. But these are never adequate or decisive. Their worth is demonstrated only by what flows from their use.

Unfortunately, the consequences emerge only after the choice of measures is made. Why, then, can't the choice of means be guided and determined by the lessons drawn from the accumulated consequences of the past? Although Dewey doesn't rule these out, he does not give them decisive weight. For the pragmatist no amount of predetermination is ever definitive; determination comes only after the act and only for that particular act.

This is a preposterous viewpoint. It dismisses as negligible the fact that everything which is determined after the fact thereupon becomes transformed into something determined before the next fact. Nothing remains indefinitely in the purely provisional state that Dewey's logic demands. When enough predeterminate material factors are piled up, the direction and outcome of developments can be foreseen.

Are social laws relative or absolute?

Compare Dewey's out-of-this-world logic with the materialistic logic of Marxism, which conforms to the real course of development and state of affairs.

Every law, including the most necessary and universal, is limited by the nature of the reality it deals with and by its own nature as a human and historically developed formulation. These give it a relative and conditional character. But that is only one aspect of its content. If the law is true, it is absolute for the processes and phenomena covered in the area of its operation.

For example, in the case under discussion, the laws of the class struggle are valid only under the conditions of class society. Before primitive society was divided into classes, these laws were not only inapplicable but unthinkable. At the other end of the historical process, as class society disappears in the socialist future, these laws will gradually lose their field of operation and wither at the roots.

Thus these laws governing social relations are both relative and absolute in their application. Their relativity is based upon the changing and contradictory course of social evolution from primitive collectivism through civilization on to socialism. Their absolutism is based upon the central role that the antagonism of class interests plays in the structure and activity of civilized society.

The material determinism of class aims

Dewey agrees that the realities of social life have to be the starting point and the foundation of any genuine morality bound up with effective social action. This means that, in a society split by antagonisms, it must be recognized that different moral demands will be invoked and different moral judgments enforced by contending classes. If this fundamental fact is waved aside, the resultant morality is bound to be fictitious or hypocritical, and any behavior in acccord with its prescriptions will give bad results.

Dewey understood that the individual functions in a given social-economic framework and that individual morality is bound up with public codes of conduct. For him social ends are ultimately decisive in moral matters. But what conditions actually do, and what ought to, decide what means will produce the desired ends? Dewey taught that informed or "creative intelligence" has to step in and do the job.

Without disputing this, it still does not answer the all-important question. What determines how people behave in this society and what kind of behavior is intelligent and creative? Here the real relations of classes and their roles in capitalist society are determinative.

The ends of classes, and of their members and movements, are actually determined by their material needs and interests. These arise from the parts they play in social production and their stake in specific forms of property. Thus the collective end of the capitalist class in the United States is to preserve and extend their economic system. That is their primary end. And it *determines* the conduct of persons belonging to that class, just as it *conditions* the lives of everyone in our society.

But the workers functioning in the same system have quite different ends, whether they are individually or fully aware of the fact or not. They are impelled by the very necessities of their living and working conditions under capitalism to try and curb their exploitation. In the long run they will be obliged to abolish its source: the private ownership of the means of production and exchange. In this struggle they have the right to use whatever means of combat they can devise for such worthy purposes. These weapons range from unionism to strike action, from political organization to social revolution.

The clash of incompatible ends determines the means employed by the contending forces. Unionism begets anti-unionism; strike-making provokes strike-breaking. Faced with mass revolutionary political action with socialist objectives the capitalist rulers discard bourgeois democracy and resort to military dictatorship or fascism. The historical course of struggle leads toward the final show-down in which one of the decisive polar classes emerges victorious over the other. Marxists consciously work for the supremacy of the working people.

These class ends are definite and clear, even if they are not always grasped or stated with precision by the representatives of capital and labor who are obliged to act in accordance with them by the environing circumstances of their socioeconomic situations, as these develop from one stage to the next.

The role of middle class liberalism
But what is the objective historical end of the middle classes and of such of their intellectual representatives as Dewey? In the domain of theory their function is to

deny the crucial importance of the class struggle, its necessity and its fruitfulness if properly organized and directed. In practice, they usually strive to curb its development by the working class while its enemies remain unrestrained and powerful. This is a hopelessly reactionary task in social science, politics, economics — and morality.

In his choice of means and in his obscuring of ends, Dewey fulfilled a specific social function as a philosophical representative of those liberal middle class elements who aspire to be the supreme mediators and moderators of class conflict in our society. In their choice of means and ends the revolutionary Marxists for whom Trotsky spoke likewise fulfill their role as champions of the fundamental, long-range interests of the working masses. The means and ends of both, in principle and in practice, are determined by their class functions and allegiances.

Many liberal moralizers contended that, if means were justified only through their usefulness in achieving ends, the most vicious practices were licensed and the gates opened to the totalitarian abominations of Stalinism. Trotsky met this argument by answering that all means were not proper in the class struggle but only those which really lead to the liberation of mankind.

"Permissible and obligatory are those and only those means, we answer, which unite the revolutionary proletariat, fill their hearts with irreconcilability to oppression, teach them contempt for official morality and its democratic echoers, imbue them with consciousness of their own historic mission, raise their courage and spirit of self-sacrifice in the struggle."

The claim of the pragmatic liberals that their morality is superior to that of the Marxists in theory and practice cannot be sustained. Their ethics lacks a sound scientific basis because it systematically disregards the most fundamental factor in the shaping of social relations and the motivating of individual conduct in modern life: the division and conflict of classes. Their moral injunctions are rendered ineffectual by failure to recognize these social realities. This not only hinders them from promoting the praiseworthy ideals of equality, cooperativeness, and peace they aspire to. Their blindness to the facts of life actually helps to reinforce reaction by restraining and disorienting the main counterforces against the evils of the existing system from taking the right road.

This is apparent nowadays when liberals and pacifists "impartially" condemn the terrorism of white supremacists and censure the measures of self-defense employed by Negroes against such attacks. This is part and parcel of the same moral-political position which places the aggressive violence of Washington on a par with the revolutionary actions of the Congolese, Dominican, and Vietnamese peoples in their anti-imperialist struggles for freedom, unity, independence, and social progress. Such false judgments come from applying abstract moral codes and categorical universals of conduct to real historical situations instead of analyzing the specific class interests and political objectives of the contending sides.

The revolutionary morality of scientific socialism is effective and progressive because it equips the laboring masses with the kind of outlook and values they need for emancipation. It generalizes and vindicates in theory their feelings that the cause they strive for is just. It explains the aims of their efforts and illuminates the kind of means required for their realization. In the simple words of the ancient moralist: "Ye shall know the truth and the truth shall make you free."

July 26, 1965

Appendices

Trotsky's exchange with Victor Serge

Appendix One:
Prospectus of 1939
French Edition

[The following is a translation of the promotional prospectus (Priere d'inserer) put out by Editions du Sagittaire for the 1939 edition of *Their Morals and Ours.*]

This deals with a very recently written book.

For Trotsky, there is no such thing as morality per se, no ideal of eternal morality. Morals are relative to each society, to each epoch, relative especially to the interests of social classes.

At the present time, most countries live under bourgeois morality. In countries where liberal democracy rules, the interests of the bourgeoisie are masked under an ideal morality, conforming, of course, to the interests of the bourgeoisie.

True morality must defend the interests of humanity itself, represented by the proletariat. Trotsky is of the opinion that his party, once in power and now in opposition, has always represented the genuine proletariat, and he, himself — genuine morality.

From this he concludes, for instance, the following: Shooting of hostages assumes an entirely different meaning depending upon whether the order is issued by Stalin or Trotsky or by the bourgeoisie. Such an order is morally valid if its aim and its tactical result is the revolutionary victory of the proletariat. Thus, Trotsky *defends* the decree that he enacted in 1919 authorizing the hostage system (wives and children of the enemy), but he condemns as *abominable* that same system when it is applied by Stalin (who, for instance, threatens the family of a diplomat whom Stalin wants to return to Russia), because Stalin acts that way to defend the bureaucracy against the proletariat.

Trotsky, basing himself on Lenin, declares that *the end jus-*

97

tifies the means (on condition that the means are effective: for example, individual terrorism is generally ineffective). There is no cynicism in this attitude, declares the author, merely a statement of facts. And it is to these facts that Trotsky says he owes his acute conscience, which constitutes his *moral sense.*

The content of this work is undoubtedly not entirely new, but never has it been expressed with such clarity nor formulated so definitively. For an entire group of intellectuals and writers of the left, deceit and violence in themselves are always bad things, from which can come only evil. For Trotsky, deceit and violence, if they are placed in the service of a justified end, should be employed without hesitation, and then, contrariwise, they represent the good.

Appendix Two:
Victor Serge's Denial
and Protest

[The British periodical *Peace News* of December 27, 1963, published an article by Victor Serge entitled "Secrecy and Revolution — A Reply to Trotsky." In a prefatory note, the editor explained that the article had been found among Serge's papers by Peter Sedgwick, translator and editor of *Memoirs of a Revolutionary 1901 — 41*; that it was not known where, if anywhere, the article had previously been published; and that it probably had been written in 1939 after the appearance of the attack on Serge in Trotsky's article "The Moralists and Sycophants Against Marxism." The following is an excerpt from Serge's article.]

"Trotsky reproaches me with being the 'severest critic' of his little book *Their Morals and Ours,* which I translated into French for Editions du Sagittaire. *However, I have never published a single line concerning that work of his, in any publication or in any shape or form.* [Emphasis in the original.]

"Trotsky credits me with the authorship of the publicity copy accompanying the distribution of his booklet to the press. On this matter, too, much to my own vexation, I must reply to him with a categoric denial. I am not the author of this prospectus; I have had no part, direct or indirect, in composing it; I have no idea who the author is; and I do not care either. Is that clear enough? Before running these false imputations to the length of five columns of argument, Trotsky would have been wise to make enquiries from the publishers, from myself or from other competent persons. The most elementary accuracy would have demanded this."

Appendix Three:
Trotsky's Reply

[That Trotsky was informed of Victor Serge's denial and protest, in a letter dated August 9, 1939, is evident from the following article translated from the Russian-language *Biulleten Oppozitsii* (Bulletin of the Opposition), No. 79-80, August-September, 1939. It was entitled "Another Refutation by Victor Serge."]

In my article "The Moralists and Sycophants," I voiced a supposition — a supposition, not an assertion — that Victor Serge had taken part in the composition of the promotional prospectus for the French edition of my work *Their Morals and Ours*; if not he personally, then one of his disciples or cothinkers. The supposition that the prospectus was written by Victor Serge occurred to various comrades, independently of one another. And not by chance: the blurb constitutes a simple resume of Victor Serge's latest sermonizings.

In his letter of August 9, Victor Serge declares that he did not have anything to do with composing the blurb. I willingly accept his declaration.

But Victor Serge does not stop there. "I must add," he says, "that the entire argumentation that you thus attribute to me sharply diverges from everything I have written on the civil war and on socialist ethics in a whole series of books and articles." With this I can in no way agree. At various times Victor Serge has written various things. But I am speaking of those views which he has developed at the present time and which tend to subordinate the class struggle of the proletariat to the norms of petty-bourgeois morality.

Instead of busying himself with constant complaints and

100

purely formal refutations, Victor Serge would do well if he tried to formulate his views in concise and exact form regarding basic revolutionary tasks or at least revolutionary morality. We state in advance: He will not do it, for he does not have definite views, but rather a confused mood of uncertainty, disillusionment, dissatisfaction, and repulsion from Marxism and proletarian revolution. Falling more and more under the influence of petty-bourgeois skepticism, V. Serge contradicts himself at every step and feels dissatisfied with others who "don't understand him" and "engage in distortions." Hence his unending refutations, devoid of any political content whatsoever.

Coyoacan, September 7, 1939   Leon Trotsky

Glossary

Amsterdam International (International Federation of Trade Unions)—founded by Social Democratic trade union officials; disappeared with advent of World War II.

Austro-Marxism—brand of reformist politics practiced by Austrian Social Democratic Party, led by Otto Bauer and Friedrich Adler.

Azana, Manuel (1880-1939)—prime minister of Spanish republican government in 1931 and again in 1936; president of republic from May 1936 until 1939.

Basch, Victor (1863-1944)—head of League for the Rights of Man in France.

Bauer, Otto (1882-1938)—leader of Austrian Social Democratic Party and theoretician of Austro-Marxism.

Bentham, Jeremy (1748-1832)—English exponent of the philosophy of utilitarianism.

Berdyaev, Nikolai A. (1874-1948)—reactionary idealist and mystic; claimed in his early writings to be influenced by Marxism.

Bernstein, Eduard (1850-1932)—German Social Democrat; after 1896 the leading exponent of what he called evolutionary socialism; supporter of class collaboration.

Bismarck, Otto von (1815-1898)—head of Prussian government 1862-71; unified Germany under Prussian hegemony; first chancellor of German empire 1871-90; introduced antisocialist law of 1878.

Blum, Léon (1872-1950)—leader of French Socialist Party; premier of People's Front government 1936-37.

Bolshevism—revolutionary political current organized by V.I. Lenin in 1903 during struggle with Mensheviks in Russian Social Democratic Labor Party; the Bolsheviks organized victory of October Revolution in 1917; changed name to Communist Party in 1918.

Bonapartism—a regime that originates in a period of social crisis and concentrates executive power in the hands of a "strong man"; the Bonapartist leader presents himself as standing above contending class forces, with aim of maintaining the power of the dominant social class or layer; term originates from the regime of Louis-Napoleon Bonaparte in France, 1852-70.

Brandler, Heinrich (1881-1967)—leader of German Communist Party in 1920s; expelled from CP in 1929; leader of right opposition to Stalin-led Communist International in 1930s.

Brockway, Fenner (1890-1988)—leader of Independent Labour Party in Britain; secretary of London Bureau; opponent of Fourth International.

Bulgakov, Sergei (1871-1944)—claimed influence by Marxism during 1890s; later became bourgeois economist and idealist philosopher.

Centrists — term used by Marxists for tendencies in workers' movement that vacillate between reformism and revolution.

Chamberlain, Neville (1869-1940)—British Conservative Party prime minister 1937-40; signer of 1938 Munich pact.

Cheka—abbreviated name of Soviet police force set up after October Revolution to combat counterrevolutionary terror and sabotage.

Comintern (Communist or Third International)—organized in 1919 as world revolutionary party following capitulation to imperialism by Social Democratic (Second) International; under Stalin became counterrevolutionary instrument of foreign policy and furthered interests of the privileged caste; dissolved in 1943.

D., Comrade (Walter Dauge, 1907-1944)—a leader of Belgian Trotskyist movement in 1930s; the letter referred to by Trotsky on page 46 was written March 27, 1936, and not in 1935; for the complete text see *Writings of Leon Trotsky* 1935-36 (Pathfinder, 1977), pp. 287.

Daladier, Edouard (1884-1970)—leader of bourgeois Radical Socialist Party; French premier in 1933-34 and 1938-40; signer of Munich pact.

Darwin, Charles (1809-1882)—English naturalist; founder of evolutionary biology; author of *Origin of Species.*

De Man, Hendrik (1885-1953)—leader of Social Democratic Belgian Labor Party; author of 1933 "labor plan" to end depression, which advocated that government should buy out capitalists.

Duranty, Walter (1884-1957)—*New York Times* correspondent in Moscow; apologist for Stalinism during Moscow trials.

Eastman, Max (1883-1968)—translated several of Trotsky's works;

broke with Marxism in 1930s; later an editor of *Reader's Digest.*

Engels, Frederick (1820-1895)—with Karl Marx, founder of modern communist workers' movement; the quotation cited by Trotsky on page 64 is from a letter to Eduard Bernstein written November 28, 1882.

First International (International Workingmen's Association)—founded in 1864; brought together working-class organizations in a number of European countries and North America; Marx and Engels were central leaders; faced stiff repression following defeat of Paris Commune in 1871; went into decline and dissolved in 1876.

Fischer, Louis (1896-1970)—U.S. journalist; wrote for the *Nation;* apologist for Stalinists during Moscow trials.

Fourth International—founded in 1938 at initiative of Leon Trotsky and other communists as revolutionary successor to Second and Third Internationals.

Franco, Francisco (1892-1975)—organized fascist forces that emerged victorious in Spanish Civil War in 1939; remained head of military dictatorship until his death.

Franco-Soviet pact—nonaggression pact signed in May 1935; a final communiqué expressed Stalin's approval of French rearmament policy.

Frank, Waldo (1889-1967)—U.S. writer, headed Communist Party–dominated League of American Writers, 1935-37; left CP after developing doubts concerning Moscow trials.

Gandhi, Mohandas (1869-1948)—leader of Indian independence movement; advocated pacifist civil disobedience as political strategy.

García Oliver, José (1901-1980)—Spanish anarchist who collaborated with Stalinists in repressing revolutionary workers during civil war.

GPU—Stalin's secret political police and terror squad; later became KGB.

Green, William (1873-1952)—right-wing president of American Federation of Labor, 1924-52.

Hegel, Georg Wilhelm (1770-1831)—German philosopher; his writings systematized from an idealist viewpoint the dialectical character of development in nature and society.

Hitler, Adolf (1889-1945)—head of German National Socialist Workers Party (Nazis); became head of state in Germany in 1933;

organized fascist forces to smash workers' movement and later carry out extermination campaign against Jews, Gypsies, and others; signer of Munich pact.

Independent Labour Party (ILP)—founded in 1893; was part of British Labour Party until 1931; affiliated to London Bureau in mid-1930s; rejoined Labour Party in 1939.

Jacobinism—named after radical left wing of bourgeois forces in French revolution that held power 1791-94.

Kant, Immanuel (1724-1804)—German philosopher; developed theory of ethics based on universal moral law, the "categorical imperative."

Kerensky, Alexander (1881-1970)—associated with right wing of Russian Socialist Revolutionary Party; prime minister of bourgeois Provisional Government from July 1917 until Bolshevik-led seizure of power by soviets in October.

Kirov, Sergei (1886-1934)—member of Political Bureau and head of Communist Party in Leningrad in 1930s; his assasination in December 1934 was used by Stalin as pretext for frame-up of political opponents.

Krivitsky, Walter (1899-1941)—former chief of Soviet intelligence in Western Europe; later exposed GPU operations; assassinated under mysterious circumstances.

Kronstadt rebellion—1921 uprising against Soviet rule at Kronstadt naval base; led by anarchists and hailed by Mensheviks and other counterrevolutionary forces; see *Kronstadt* (Pathfinder, 1979) for Trotsky's account.

"Labor Bank"—see De Man, Hendrik.

Largo Caballero, Francisco (1869-1946)—leader of left wing of Spanish Socialist Party; premier in Popular Front government 1936-37.

Lassalle, Ferdinand (1825-1864)—founder of General German Workers Union, which later merged with Marxists to form Social Democratic Party.

League for the Rights of Man—French civil liberties organization.

Left Opposition—formed in Soviet Union in 1923 to defend communist course of Lenin and Bolsheviks against Stalinist counterrevolution; was later organized on international scale, becoming Fourth International in 1938.

Legal Marxism—current in Russia in late 1890s that advocated gradual reforms, renounced revolutionary activity, but claimed to be influenced by Marxism; functioned legally under tsarism; its main proponents later became capitalist political figures.

Lenin, V.I. (1870-1924)—central leader of Bolshevik Party; led struggle of workers and peasants to power in 1917; chair of Council of People's Commissars 1917-24; central leader of Communist International.

Lewis, John L. (1880-1969)—president of United Mine Workers Union 1920-69; a top official of Congress of Industrial Organizations 1935-40.

Liebknecht, Karl (1871-1919)—a leader of revolutionary wing of German Social Democratic Party and opponent of World War I; a founding leader of German Communist Party; assassinated with Rosa Luxemburg by army officers instigated by Social Democratic government.

London Bureau—international grouping of centrist organizations set up in 1932 at initiative of Norwegian Labor Party and British Independent Labour Party; opposed call for Fourth International.

Lovestone, Jay (1898-1990)—leader of early U.S. Communist Party; expelled from Stalin-led CP in 1929 and formed right opposition to Communist International; later became pro-imperialist foreign policy official in AFL-CIO.

Ludendorff, Erich von (1865-1937)—German general who supported Hitler.

Ludwig, Emil (1881-1948)—German journalist; biographer of contemporary statesmen and historical figures.

Luther, Martin (1483-1546)—initiator of Protestant Reformation in Germany.

Luxemburg, Rosa (1871-1919)—leader of revolutionary wing of German Social Democratic Party; jailed in 1915 for opposing World War I; founder of German Communist Party; assassinated with Karl Liebknecht by army officers instigated by Social Democratic government.

Lyons, Eugene (1898-1985)—radical U.S. author and editor in 1920s and 1930s; broke with Marxism after becoming disillusioned by Stalinism.

Mach, Ernst (1838-1916)—Austrian positivist philosopher; exponent of antimaterialist view that world consists solely of sensations.

MacMahon, Marie Edne Patrice de (1808-1903)—French militarist and bourgeois politician; organized bloody suppression of

Paris Commune in 1871; president of France 1873-79.

Makhno, Nestor (1884-1934)—leader of Ukrainian peasant-based partisan bands during Civil War; fought both against Soviet government and against armies organized by landlords and capitalists; routed by Red Army in 1920.

Marx, Karl (1818-1883)—founder with Frederick Engels of modern communist workers' movement and leader of First International 1864-76.

Mikado—title given to emperor of Japan; held by Hirohito 1926-89.

Mill, John Stuart (1806-1873)—English economist and positivist philosopher, shared utilitarian views of Jeremy Bentham, but took stronger stand in favor of reform movements.

Molinier, Raymond (1904-   )—supporter of Left Opposition in France; expelled from French organization in 1935 for violating party decisions.

Munich pact—1938 agreement signed by Germany, Italy, France, and Britain that approved German occupation of Czechoslovakia.

Mussolini, Benito (1883-1945)—former leader of Socialist Party of Italy; organized Italian fascist movement in 1919; became dictator in 1922 and organized crushing of working-class movement; signer of Munich pact.

Negrín, Juan (1889-1956)—last premier of Spanish Republican government, replacing Largo Caballero in May 1937; resigned in 1939.

Nikolaev, Leonid (1904-1934)—young opponent of Stalin's regime who assassinated Sergei Kirov in 1934; tried in secret and executed.

Norwegian Labor Party—affiliated with London Bureau, later returning to Second International; in 1935 became governing party of Norway and granted asylum to Trotsky; under Soviet pressure interned Trotsky for four months after first Moscow trial, finally deporting him to Mexico at end of 1936.

Oak, Liston (1895-1970)—U.S. journalist; Stalinist until 1937; wrote for Trotskyist press briefly before shifting to Social Democracy.

October Revolution (1917)—Bolshevik-led insurrection that brought Russian workers and peasants to power; it followed February 1917 revolution that abolished tsarism and instituted bourgeois coalition government.

Paris Commune (1871)—first attempt to establish revolutionary government of the toilers; working people held power from March 18 to May 28; crushed by troops of bourgeois government, who massacred more than 17,000.

Paz, Magdeleine (1889-1973)—supporter of Left Opposition in 1920s; broke with Marxism and became active in French civil liberties work in 1930s.

People's Front (Popular Front)—name given in 1935 to coalition of French workers' parties with bourgeois Radical Party; political strategy that was put forward by Comintern after 1935 of subordinating political independence and program of workers' parties to coalitions with liberal capitalist parties.

Pivert, Marceau (1895-1958)—served as aide to French Popular Front government in 1936-37; left Socialist Party to set up centrist Workers and Peasants Socialist Party (PSOP); later rejoined SP.

POUM (Workers Party of Marxist Unification)—left-centrist socialist organization during Spanish Civil War; signed popular front pact and joined in bourgeois government in 1936; outlawed and suppressed in 1937 at instigation of Stalinists.

Pritt, Denis N. (1888-1972)—successful lawyer, uncritical admirer of Stalin; member of British Parliament, 1935-50.

Rappoport, Charles (1865-1941)—Russian revolutionist; emigrated to France and became leader of Socialist Party and later a founding leader of French communist movement; broke with Communist Party in 1938 and rejoined SP in 1940.

Rolland, Romain (1866-1944)—leading French writer; pacifist in World War I; apologist for Stalinism from late 1930s.

Rosenmark, Raymond (1885-1950)—French attorney; in 1936 wrote special "report" for French League for the Rights of Man that was a gross apology for first Moscow trial.

Second International (Social Democracy or Socialist International)—organized in 1889 as successor to First International; collapsed during World War I when most of its national sections supported their respective capitalist governments; reorganized on class-collaborationist foundation in 1923.

Sedov, Leon (1906-1938)—Trotsky's older son; a leader of Left Opposition; assassinated by GPU in Paris.

Serge, Victor (1890-1947)—writer and novelist; active in anarchist movement prior to World War I; moved to Soviet Union and worked for Comintern following October Revolution; arrested in

1933 as Left Oppositionist but freed in 1936 as a result of campaign in France; moved to France where he broke with Fourth International.

Shaftesbury, Anthony (1671-1713)—English philosopher, moralist, and student of John Locke; hypothesized existence of "moral sense" to reconcile individual happiness with general welfare.

Sixty Families—term coined by Ferdinand Lundberg, author of *America's Sixty Families* (1937), which lists families who own bulk of wealth in U.S.

Sneevliet, Henk (1883-1942)—founder of Marxist movement in Indonesia and leader of Dutch Communist Party and Left Opposition; broke with Fourth International in 1938; executed by Nazis in World War II.

Socialist Party (France)—French section of the Second International and part of the Popular Front.

Social Revolutionaries (Socialist Revolutionary Party)—main peasant-supported party in Russia during 1917 revolution; its left wing formed coalition government with Bolsheviks following October Revolution, but later went into armed opposition.

Souvarine, Boris (1893-1984)—founder of French Communist Party; expelled in 1924 for support of Left Opposition; rejected communism in 1930s.

Spaak, Paul-Henri (1899-1972)—briefly in left wing of Belgian Labor Party in early 1930s; became minister in Belgian cabinet in 1935; secretary general of North Atlantic Treaty Organization (NATO) in 1950s.

Spencer, Herbert (1820-1903)—English philosopher and advocate of individualism; distorted Darwin's biological theory into a unifying principle of his own social philosophy.

Stalin, Joseph (1879-1953)—member of Bolshevik Central Committee in 1912; Lenin called for his removal as general secretary of Communist Party in 1923; after Lenin's death presided over bureaucratic degeneration of Russian CP and Comintern; organized Moscow trials in 1930s and murder of majority of Bolshevik leaders of Lenin's time.

Struve, Peter B. (1870-1944)—founding member of Russian Social Democracy in 1893; subsequently became a liberal who claimed to be influenced by Marxism; after 1905 lined up with right wing and opposed October 1917 revolution; leading supporter of forces that fought to restore landlords and capitalists during civil war.

Tell, William—popular legendary figure of Swiss patriotism; allegedly began revolt against Habsburg rule in 1291.

Thermidor—month in French revolutionary calendar when radical Jacobins were overthrown, opening up period of reaction that could not, however, reinstitute feudal regime toppled by French Revolution; Trotsky used term as historical analogy to designate seizure of power by Stalinist bureaucracy within framework of nationalized property relations established in 1918 following October Revolution.

Thomas, Norman (1884-1968)—leader of U.S. Socialist Party; six-time candidate for president.

Thorez, Maurice (1900-1964)—general secretary of French Communist Party 1930-64.

Tolstoy, Leo (1828-1910)—Russian novelist; developed extreme ascetic, religious, and pacifist views in later years.

Tranmael, Martin (1879-1967)—longtime leader of Norwegian Labor Party.

Tukhachevsky, Mikhail (1893-1937)—a central Soviet military leader during civil war; appointed marshal of USSR in 1933; executed by Stalin.

Utilitarianism—philosophical doctrine of rising British industrial bourgeoisie associated with Jeremy Bentham, James Mill, and John Stuart Mill.

Vandervelde, Emile (1866-1938)—Belgian right-wing Social Democrat; president of Second International 1929-36.

Vereecken, Georges (1896-1978)—leader of sectarian tendency of Left Opposition in Belgium in 1930s.

Versailles government—French regime headed by Adolphe Thiers in 1871 that fled during Paris Commune; returned later that year after brutal suppression of Commune.

Vorlander, Karl (1860-1919)—German philosopher; attempted to combine socialism with Kantianism.

Vyshinsky, Andrei (1883-1954)—chief prosecutor in Moscow trials; Soviet foreign minister 1949-53.

Walcher, Jacob (1887-1970)—a founder of German Communist Party; expelled in 1929 as supporter of right opposition; led centrist German Socialist Workers Party and opposed formation of Fourth International; rejoined CP after World War II.

Wells, H.G. (1866-1946)—English novelist, sociological writer, and historian.

Wrangel, Pyotr (1878-1928)—general in tsarist army and commander-in-chief of counterrevolutionary forces in south Russia 1919-20; fled country after defeat by Red Army.

Yagoda, Genrikh (1891-1938)—headed GPU 1934-36; organized first Moscow trial; executed after third Moscow trial.

Yakir, Yona (1896-1937)—joined Bolsheviks in April 1917; Soviet general; arrested and executed during Stalin purges.

Yezhov, Nikolai (1894-1939?)—replaced Yagoda as head of GPU; disappeared after third Moscow trial.

Zenzinov, Vladimir (1880-1953)—joined Socialist Revolutionary Party in 1900; elected to Constituent Assembly in 1917; left Russia following October Revolution.

Index

Absolutes, 53, 61, 73, 76-77, 89
"Amoralism" of Bolsheviks, 15, 26-27, 33, 35, 42-45, 47, 62
Amsterdam International and Moscow trials, 30
Anarchists, 13; and Stalinists, 29, 31, 42
Anti-Dühring, 77
Austro-Marxism, 30
Azana, Manuel, 56

Basch, Victor, 61
Bauer, Otto, 30
Bentham, Jeremy, 19
Berdyaev, Nikolai, 17
Bernstein, Eduard, 60-61
Bismarck, Otto von, 50
Blum, Léon, 30, 34
Bolshevism, 9, 25, 61-62; and czarism, 13, 15; and Jesuitism, 18; and Stalinism, 10
Bonapartism, 32
Brandler, Heinrich, 31
Brockway, Fenner, 31
Bulgakov, Sergei, 17

Caballero. *See* Largo Caballero, Francisco
Categorical imperative, 22, 61
Catholicism, 53-54, 78
Centrists, 40, 60
Chamberlain, Neville, 66

Cheka, 58
Civil war: in America, 38; in Russia, 7; in Spain, 55
Class struggle, 20, 56, 81; and deductive method, 70-73, 82; and dialectics, 52; laws of, 84, 90-91; and morality of civil war, 36-37, 58-59; and question of hostages, 37-40, 54-57; and question of means and ends, 14, 20, 88-90; as viewed by liberals, 83
Comintern. *See* Communist International
Commandments, 21-22
Commission of Inquiry. *See* Dewey, John, and Commission of Inquiry
Common Sense, 15, 25
Common sense, 22, 24-26
Communist International, 8 and Moscow trials, 30
Communist Party (Germany), 8
Croix, 53, 56

D. *See* Dauge, Walter
Daladier, Edouard, 66
Darwin, Charles, 17, 19-20
Dauge, Walter (Comrade D.), 46
De Man, Hendrick, 46, 54
Deduction, 82
Dewey, John: on class struggle,

New International
A MAGAZINE OF MARXIST POLITICS AND THEORY

IN ISSUE 7

OPENING GUNS OF WORLD WAR III
Washington's Assault on Iraq
Jack Barnes

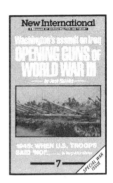

The U.S. government's murderous bombardment and invasion of Iraq heralds a period of increasingly sharp conflicts among imperialist powers, new wars, and crises of the world capitalist system.

1945: WHEN U.S. TROOPS SAID 'NO'!
Mary-Alice Waters

LESSONS FROM THE IRAN-IRAQ WAR
Samad Sharif

$12.00

IN ISSUE 8

CHE GUEVARA, CUBA, AND THE ROAD TO SOCIALISM

An exchange of views on the relationship of the working class, internationalism, communist leadership, and the construction of socialism.

$10.00

IN ISSUE 3

COMMUNISM AND THE FIGHT FOR A POPULAR REVOLUTIONARY GOVERNMENT
Mary-Alice Waters   *$8.00*

IN ISSUE 6

WASHINGTON'S 50-YEAR DOMESTIC CONTRA OPERATION
Larry Seigle   *$10.00*

Order from Pathfinder, see front of book for distributors.

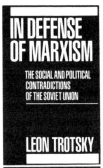

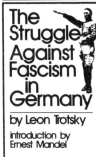

America's Revolutionary Heritage

edited by George Novack

Explanatory essays on Native Americans, the first American revolution, the Civil War, the rise of industrial capitalism, and the first wave of the fight for women's rights. 414 pp., $20.95

Understanding History

George Novack

Why understanding history is a political necessity in the working-class fight for socialism. 208 pages, $14.95

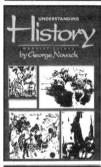

The Case of Leon Trotsky

Hearings of the 1937 Dewey Commission on Stalin's charges against Trotsky in the Moscow trials. Cloth, 617 pages, $70.00

Not Guilty

Report of the Commission of Inquiry chaired by John Dewey into the charges made against Leon Trotsky in the Moscow trials. Cloth, 422 pages, $60.00

Trade Unions in the Epoch of Imperialist Decay

Leon Trotsky, Karl Marx

Two revolutionary working-class leaders discuss the tasks of unions and their relationship to the struggle for economic justice and political power. 156 pages, $13.95

Available from Pathfinder. See front of book for distributors.

Further Reading

The Communist Manifesto
Karl Marx and Frederick Engels, $2.50

The Changing Face of U.S. Politics
The Proletarian Party and the Trade Unions
Jack Barnes, $18.95

Teamster Rebellion
Farrell Dobbs, $14.95

Notebook of an Agitator
James P. Cannon, $19.95

Democracy and Revolution
George Novack, $17.95

In Defense of Socialism
Fidel Castro, $12.95

Sexism and Science
Evelyn Reed, $14.95

Che Guevara and the Cuban Revolution
Writings and Speeches of Ernesto Che Guevara,
$20.95

Malcolm X Talks to Young People
Malcolm X, $9.95

Abortion Is a Woman's Right
Pat Grogan and others, $2.50

The Struggle Is My Life
Nelson Mandela, $12.95

How Far We Slaves Have Come!
South Africa and Cuba in Today's World
Nelson Mandela and Fidel Castro, $7.95